OUT OF YOUR SEAT ON YOUR FEET AND IN THE STREETS

979-8-9866536-6-2

Designed & Published by JWG Publishing House.
Printed in the United States of America.

Table of Contents

CHAPTER 1

THE BOOK OF EZRA

Ezra continues the Old Testament narrative of Second Chronicles by showing how God fulfills His promise to return His people to the land of promise after seventy years of exile. Israel's "second exodus" this one from Babylon, is less impressive than the return from Egypt because only a remnant (small quantity) chooses to leave Babylon. Ezra relates the story of two returns from Babylon; the first one was led by Zerubbabel to rebuild the temple in chapters one through six, and the second, under the leadership of Ezra, to rebuild the spiritual condition of the people in chapters seven through the tenth chapter. Ezra and Nehemiah were originally bound together as one book because Chronicles, Ezra, and Nehemiah were viewed as one continuous history. Ezra is the writer of this book, and as a priest he was unable to serve during the captivity. There was no temple because it had been destroyed. He did, however, remain focused and gave quality time to study the Word of God. Ezra Chapter seven verse six, says:

“This Ezra came up from Babylon; and he was a skilled scribe in the Law of Moses, which the “LORD God of Israel had given. The king granted him all his requests, according to the hand of the “LORD, his God upon him.”

Ezra 7:6 NKJV

The preceding verse lets us know that Ezra was "a ready scribe in the law of Moses" In the Book of Nehemiah it also shows us that Ezra was a great revivalist according to the following scripture.

" So, they read distinctly from the book, in the Law of God; and they gave the sense and helped them to understand the reading. And Nehemiah, who was the governor; Ezra, the priest and scribe; and the Levites, who taught the people, said to all the people.

“This day is holy to the “LORD your God; do not mourn nor weep.” For all the people wept, when they heard the words of the Law.”

Nehemiah 8:8-9 NKJV

Ezra was the organizer of the synagogue and the founding order of the scribes. According to the following ten scriptures, the theme of the book of Ezra is the "The Word of the “Lord"

1.“Now in the first year of Cyrus king of Persia, that the word of the “LORD by the mouth of Jeremiah might be fulfilled, the “LORD stirred up the spirit of Cyrus king of Persia, so that he made a proclamation throughout all his kingdom, and also put it in writing, saying,"

Ezra 1:1 NKJV

2."Then Jeshua the son of Jozadak and his brethren the priests, and Zerubbabel the son of Shealtiel and his brethren, arose and built the altar of the God of Israel, to offer burnt offerings on it, as it is written in the Law of Moses the man of God."

Ezra 3:2 NKJV

3."So the elders of the Jews built, and they prospered through the prophesying of Haggai the prophet and Zechariah, the son of Iddo. And they built and finished it, according to the commandment of the God of Israel, and according to the commandment of Cyrus, Darius, and Artaxerxes king of Persia."

Ezra 6:14 NKJV

4."They assigned the priests to their divisions, and the Levites to their divisions, over the service of God in Jerusalem, as it is written in the Book of Moses."

Ezra 6:18 NKJV

5."this Ezra came up from Babylon; and he was a skilled scribe in the Law of Moses, which the "LORD God of Israel had given. The king granted him all his requests, according to the hand of the "LORD his God upon him."

Ezra 7:6 NKJV

6."For Ezra had prepared his heart to seek the Law of the "LORD, and to do it, and to teach statutes and ordinances in Israel."

Ezra 7:10 NKJV

7."And whereas you are being sent by the king and his seven counselors to inquire concerning Judah and Jerusalem, with regard to the Law of your God which is in your hand;"

Ezra 7:14 NKJV

8."Then everyone who trembled at the words of the God of Israel assembled to me, because of the transgression of those who had been carried away captive, and I sat astonished until the evening sacrifice."

Ezra 9:4 NKJV

9."Now therefore, let us make a covenant with our God to put away all these wives and those who have been born to them, according to the advice of my master and of those who tremble at the commandment of our God; and let it be done according to the law."

Ezra 10:3 NKJV

10."Then Ezra arose, and made the leaders of the priests, the Levites, and all Israel swear an oath that they would do according to this word. So, they swore an oath."

Ezra 10:5 NKJV

The main scriptures of the book of Ezra are, Ezra 9:4 and 10:3. However, when you read and study 2 Chronicles, it talks about how the southern kingdom of Judah went into captivity for seventy years. After this captivity we don't hear about these kingdoms or the captives until Ezra picks up history. There are three historical books that are called "post captivity" books: Ezra, Nehemiah, and Esther. Also, there are three prophetical "post captivity" books: Haggai, Zechariah, and Malachi. The books of Ezra and Nehemiah belong together. Ezra was a priest and Nehemiah was a layman. They worked together to make sure that God's work was accomplished in Jerusalem. Together they made sure that the walls, the city of Jerusalem and the temple were rebuilt. Haggai and Zechariah also work together. They encouraged the people to build the temple. As you read the book of Ezra, you will see that Haggai was a very practical man. The reconstruction and refurbishing of the temple were his passion. Zechariah was a dreamer. I would like to say it this way, "while Haggai was doing the ground attack Zechariah was doing the air attack". Zechariah did not concern himself with the foundation under the temple, or with the measurements and doors of the temple. Haggai and Zechariah were a team just like Ezra and Nehemiah. As you read and study the Book of Ezra, I would strongly suggest you also read and study the Books of Haggai and Zechariah. All three books were written during the rebuilding of the temple.

"Then the prophet Haggai and Zechariah the son of Iddo, prophets, prophesied to the Jews who were in Judah and Jerusalem, in the name of the God of Israel, who was over them."

Ezra 5:1 NKJV

In the Book of Ezra there are two major divisions. The first division is the first six chapters talks about the return of the captives from Babylon, led by Zerubbabel, which were about fifty thousand who returned. The second division is the last four chapters that talk about the return of the two-thousand people who followed Ezra.

DECREE OF CYRUS FOR THE TEMPLE RESTORATION

Notice immediately, Ezra puts an emphasis on the Word of God. He mentions Cyrus, the King of Persia. He was one of the most direct rulers of the ancient world. He was the subject of predictive prophecy; he was named before he was born almost two hundred years before his coming as king of Persia.

"Who says of Cyrus, 'He is My shepherd, and he shall perform all My pleasure, saying to Jerusalem, "You shall be built." And to the temple, "Your foundation shall be laid."

Isaiah 44:28 NKJV

""Thus says the "LORD to His anointed, To Cyrus, whose right hand I have held— To subdue nations before him and loose the armor of kings, to open before him the double doors, so that the gates will not be shut:"

Isaiah 45:1 NKJV

Cyrus was a type of Christ. Daniel was a prime minister in the court of Cyrus, and shared with him the knowledge of God. Cyrus knew what he was doing when he made a decree proclaiming that the nation of Israel could return to their land, and the will of the "Lord would be fulfilled. The seventy years of captivity was over, the decree was given, and the children of Israel could return to their land. The decree of Cyrus is very important, he had been given all the kingdoms of the earth. The expression in the verse says, "The "Lord God of Heaven", this shows a destination of God which is vitally important to Ezra, Nehemiah, and Daniel. Why? Because after the fall of Jerusalem and the destruction of Jerusalem, God could no longer be identified with the temple as the One who dwelled between the cherubims. The glory had departed. Ezekiel saw the vision of God's Glory departing from the temple at Jerusalem. There was a pause to see if the people of God would return to Him and turn away from their idolatry; but they did not. The Shekinah Glory went over the city, rested on the top of the Mount of Olives, and waited again, but there was still no turning to God. That was when the glory went back to heaven, and was not seen again. Although the Shekinah glory was not visible. It was veiled in human flesh. He was God. He had laid aside his glory when he came to earth, but he was one-hundred percent God and man. Because his glory was veiled, He was rejected and crucified. In the Gospel of Matthew, He was born as a king. He lived like a king. He performed miracles as a king. He taught as a king. He was arrested as a king. He was tried as a king. He died as a king. He was buried as a king. He then rose as a king and went back to heaven as a king. When the Shekinah glory was removed from the earth, God gave His people into the hands of the Gentiles and sent them into Babylonian captivity. Let's now look at the second verse of Ezra. ", "Thus says Cyrus king of Persia: All the kingdoms of the earth, the "LORD God of heaven has given me. And He has commanded me to build Him a house at Jerusalem which is in Judah."

Ezra 1:2 NKJV

It says, "He has commanded me to build him a house at Jerusalem" The reason this is good is that Cyrus was a Gentile world ruler at the time. Remember Cyrus, through the ministry of Daniel the prophet, shared the Gospel with him. Cyrus now gives permission for the Jews who had been in Babylonian captivity to return to Jerusalem.

"Who is among you of all His people? May his God be with him, and let him go up to Jerusalem, which is in Judah, and build the house of the "LORD God of Israel (He is God), which is in Jerusalem."

Ezra 1:3 NKJV

Notice that God has commanded Cyrus to do this; but Cyrus did not command the people to go to Jerusalem; he granted them permission to go up.

"And whoever is left in any place where he dwells, let the men of his place help him with silver and gold, with goods and livestock, besides the freewill offerings for the house of God which is in Jerusalem."

Ezra 1:4 NKJV

Permission was granted to the people to return, but they chose not to. They wanted to make an offering of gold, silver and other things of value. However, the only command was to rebuild the temple at Jerusalem.

"Then the heads of the fathers' houses of Judah and Benjamin, and the priests and the Levites, with all whose spirits God had moved, arose to go up and build the house of the "LORD which is in Jerusalem. And all those who were around them encouraged them with articles of silver and gold; with goods and livestock, and with precious things, besides all that was willingly offered."

Ezra 1:5-6 NKJV

There was only a small percentage of the people who went up. Maybe they had a good excuse for their reason for not going up. It was God's will for them to go up, but some chose not to do so; they had settled down in Babylon. Maybe they were enjoying the comfort of the society of Babylon. Many of them had become prosperous, so they chose not to go up. They felt that it was not God's will or the time for them to go up. I'm not saying that they were out of the will of God but one thing I know for sure, is that in the book of Esther it talks about those who remained in the land, and at that time they were out of the will of God. Something that I have noticed about these two groups of people is, there was no spirit of judgment between the two groups (those who returned and those who did not). The group that remained helped the group that went up as they provided the essentials they needed. Now, in Ezra's day, the people who did not return felt a responsibility to become partners with the group that went back to Jerusalem. The group that returned was of the poorer class. They were the chief of the fathers of Judah, Benjamin; the priests, and the Levites.

"King Cyrus also brought out the articles of the house of the "LORD, which Nebuchadnezzar had taken from Jerusalem and put in the temple of his Gods."

Ezra 1:7 NKJV

How did Cyrus get the vessels of the house of the Lord?

While he tasted the wine, Belshazzar gave the command to bring the gold and silver vessels which his father Nebuchadnezzar, had taken from the temple. These had been in Jerusalem; the king and his lords, his wives, and his concubines were to drink from them. Then they brought the gold vessels that had been taken from the temple of the house of God, and had been in Jerusalem. The king and his lords, his wives, and his concubines drank from them. They drank wine, and praised the Gods of gold and silver, bronze and iron, wood and stone."

Daniel 5:2-4 NKJV

That very night the city of Babylon was captured. The Persian Kings had put away these vessels; so when Cyrus became king, they were there. Now these holy vessels (holy in the sense that they were used for the glory of God) were put back into the hands of the priests and Levites who returned to Jerusalem.

"This is the number of them: thirty gold platters; one thousand silver platters; twenty, twenty-nine knives, thirty gold basins, four hundred and ten silver basins of a similar kind, and one thousand other articles. All the articles of gold and silver were five thousand four hundred. All these Sheshbazzar took with them the captives, who were brought from Babylon to Jerusalem."

Ezra 1:9-11 NKJV

RETURN UNDER ZERUBBABEL

"Now these are the people of the province who came back from the captivity, of those who had been carried away, whom Nebuchadnezzar the king of Babylon had carried away to Babylon, and who returned to Jerusalem and Judah, everyone to his own city. Those who came with Zerubbabel were Jeshua, Nehemiah, Seraiah,

Reelaiah, Mordecai, Bilshan, Mispar, Bigvai, Rehum, and Baanah. The number of the men of the people of Israel:"

Ezra 2:1-2 NKJV

Chapter two will give us a list of those who returned to Jerusalem under the leadership of Zerubbabel. After the captivity they really became difficult because there was the inclusion of that which was of the Persian and Babylonian languages. Did you notice that in verse two a man named Nehemiah was mentioned? This was not the Nehemiah that wrote the book that is in Bible. Nehemiah the writer, did not return to the land with the first group. Also, noticed that Mordecai is mentioned. He is not the same man who is mentioned in the book of Esther.

"The men of Anathoth, one hundred and twenty-eight;"

Ezra 2:23 NKJV

This is the town where Jeremiah purchased a field. Remember, in Jeremiah's' day the children of Israel were on the verge of being carried way into captivity. When Jeremiah bought the land, it didn't look as though Israel had a future, but God had him buy the land as a sign that Judah would be restored. Jeremiah's action was a sign of faith in God's promises, that his people would return to the land, and they did. These men of Anathoth had a sealed, lawful claim to the land, because or the children of Israel have provoked Me only to anger with the work of their hands,' says the "LORD. 'For this city has been to Me a provocation of My anger and My fury from the day that they built it, even to this day; so I will remove it from before My face because of all the evil of the children of Israel and the children of Judah, which they have done to provoke Me to anger— they, their kings, their princes, their priests, their prophets, the men of Judah, and the inhabitants of Jerusalem. And they have turned to Me the back, and not the face; though I taught them, rising up early and teaching them; yet they have not listened to receive instruction. But they set their abominations in the house, which is called by My name, to defile it. And they built the high places of Baal, which are in the Valley of the Son of Hinnom, to cause their sons and their daughters to pass through the fire to Molech, which I did not command them, nor did it come into My mind that they should do this abomination, to cause Judah to sin.' "Now therefore, thus says the "LORD, the God of Israel, concerning this city of which you say, 'It shall be delivered into the hand of the king of Babylon by the sword, by the famine, and by the pestilence': Behold, I will gather them out of all countries where I have driven them in My anger, in My fury, and in great wrath; I will bring them back to this place, and I will cause them to dwell safely. They shall be My people, and I will be their God; then I will give them one heart and one way, that they may fear Me forever, for the good of them and their children after them. And I will make an everlasting covenant with them, that I will not turn away from doing them good; but I will put My fear in their hearts, so that they will not depart from Me. Yes, I will rejoice over them to do them good; and I will assuredly plant them in this land, with all My heart and with all My soul.' "For thus says the "LORD: 'Just as I have brought all this great calamity on this people, so I will bring on them all the good that I have promised them. And fields will be bought in this land, of which you say, "It is desolate, without man or beast; it has been given into the hand of the Chaldeans." Men will buy fields for money, sign deeds and seal them, and take witnesses, in the land of Benjamin, in the places around Jerusalem, in the cities of Judah, in the cities of the mountains, in the cities of the lowland, and in the cities of the South; for I will cause their captives to return,' says the "LORD."

Jeremiah 32:1-44 NKJV

There are at least four spiritual lessons in the text. Some rebuilt the temple; some gave out the word of God; some went as missionaries and others supported those who were on the mission field. One thing for sure, is that every person's work one day will be rewarded. All our work will be inspected with the reward in mind. Every born- again believer will appear before the judgment seat of Christ.

"For we [believers will be called to account and] must all appear before the judgment seat of Christ, so that each one may be repaid for what has been done in the body, whether good or bad [that is, each will be held responsible for his actions, purposes, goals, motives—

the use or misuse of his time, opportunities and abilities]."

2 Corinthians 5:10 AMP

"Each one's work will be clearly shown [for what it is]; for the day [of judgment] will disclose it, because it is to be revealed with fire, and the fire will test the quality and character and worth of each person's work. If any person's work which he has built [on this foundation, that is, any outcome of his effort] remains [and survives this test], he will receive a reward. But if any person's work is burned up [by the test], he will suffer the loss [of his reward]; yet he himself will be saved, but only as [one who has barely escaped] through fire."

1 Corinthians 3:13-15 AMP

"The Levites: the sons of Jeshua and Kadmiel, of the sons of Hodaviah, seventy-four. The singers: the sons of Asaph, one hundred and twenty-eight."

Ezra 2:40-41 NKJV

There were one hundred and twenty-eight singers who went back to the land. The spirit of praise and rejoicing was in their hearts and lives. They had a lot to sing about, but, more singers returned to the land than did Levites.

TEMPLE REBUILDING BEGAN AND STOPPED

This first group that returned to Jerusalem after the captivity numbered only about fifty thousand. The next delegation, led by Ezra, only about two thousand returned. There were others who came, which may have grown the population to about sixty thousand; but still there were several million Israelites at this time. You can see that the great majority remained in the land of Babylon and in the other areas, rather than returning to the promise land.

"And when the seventh month had come, and the children of Israel were in the cities, the people gathered together as one man to Jerusalem."

Ezra 3:1 NKJV

Obviously, there is a time lapse between Ezra chapters two and three. Ezra chapter two, concluded with the children of Israel returning to the land. They took an abundance of wealth with them to rebuild the temple and restore the land. During the lapse of time, they built homes because we find later that Haggai rebuked them for building their homes and neglecting the temple. The elapsed time could have been several weeks, several months, or as much as two years.

"Then Jeshua the son of Jozadak and his brethren the priests, and Zerubbabel the son of Shealtiel and his brethren, arose and built the altar of the God of Israel, to offer burnt offerings on it, as it is written in the Law of Moses the man of God."

Ezra 3:2 NKJV

They searched the scriptures and they found what was written in the Law of Moses. When they found what was written, there was no controversy or difference of opinion. They not only returned to the land, but they also returned to the Law of Moses. The Bible was their authority; therefore, neither the ideas nor the opinions of individuals entered into their decision. The scriptures are all sufficient and contain all the instructions that are needed for the guidance of those who would be faithful to God. The word of God has all the answers, so it's always good to go back to the source.

"Though fear had come upon them because of the people of those countries, they set the altar on its bases; and they offered burnt offerings on it to the "LORD, both the morning and evening burnt offerings."

Ezra 3:3 NKJV

The altar erected was the altar of burnt offering. This altar, as we have already seen, speaks of the cross of Christ. The burnt sacrifice that was offered speaks of the person of Christ and his sacrifice for us. Christ offered himself without sin to God and died for all our sins. What they were doing when they offered this sacrifice was meeting about the person of Christ and his atoning death. Every born-again believer should understand that those who have received Christ as Savior have been baptized by the Holy Spirit into the body of believers (the church). Fellowship has nothing to do with ethnicity, social status, wealth, or denomination, etc. The question is, had they received Jesus Christ in their life, is what makes all the difference, which is the most important thing.

"But many of the priests and Levites and heads of the fathers' houses, old men who had seen the first temple, wept with a loud voice when the foundation of this temple was laid before their eyes. Yet many shouted aloud for joy, so that the people could not discern the noise of the shout of joy from the noise of the weeping of the people, for the people shouted with a loud shout, and the sound was heard afar off."

Ezra 3:12-13 NKJV

There were two groups present at the dedication service. The young people who had never seen the temple of old, this was something new to them, in all their youth and enthusiasm; they were praising God and the "Lord bless them. The other group was composed of the older generation; they remember Solomon's temple and how beautiful it was. Can you imagine with the older generation was probably saying, this second temple is nothing, if those young people could only have seen Solomon's temple! "But what they were saying was not very encouraging to the younger generation, but it was true. One of the problems God had to overcome was discouragement that came because of the older generation talking the way they did. As a result, we find that Haggai the prophet told the people, "The "Lord says, "Go ahead and build because God is with you. He was not at the beautiful temple of Solomon's; at the end the glory had left it; but God is with you now go ahead and build.

There are a lot of older people from previous generations, even today that will discourage the work of God. This causes them to be held back because they only remember the old days and it's hard to grasp the new days.

ARTAXERXES DECREE STOPS REBUILDING

"Now when the adversaries of Judah and Benjamin heard that the descendants of the captivity were building the temple of the "LORD God of Israel, they came to Zerubbabel and the heads of the fathers' houses, and said to them, "Let us build with you, for we seek your God as you do; and we have sacrificed to Him since the days of Esarhaddon king of Assyria, who brought us here." But Zerubbabel and Jeshua and the rest of the heads of the fathers' houses of Israel said to them, "You may do nothing with us to build a house for our God; but we alone will build to the "LORD God of Israel, as King Cyrus, the king of Persia, has commanded us." Then the people of the land tried to discourage the people of Judah. They troubled them in building and hired counselors against them to frustrate their purpose all the days of Cyrus king of Persia, even until the reign of Darius king of Persia."

Ezra 4:1-5 NKJV

Not only did two tribes return to the land (Judah and Benjamin), but all twelve tribes went back. The people returned to the promise land during the days of

Esarhaddon, King of Assur (Assyria). It was Assyria which had taken the northern tribes captive. Some of the people had blended back into the land and had mixed with the Samaritans. As a result, they wanted to join up with those who had come from Babylon. The enemies first effort to stop the work of rebuilding the temple is to offer to become allies. The Devils job has always been to try to stop the work of God moving forward. The adversaries of Judah and Benjamin said, "We have been worshiping God here all along, and you have just returned so let us join in with you and let's worship him together. "We will see that this might sound good, but it was not genuine. The chief fathers were not nice at all. They absolutely rejected the enemies offer to become allies. The Israelites didn't seem to be interested in the movement at all; as a matter of fact, they were rude, but they were right. Verses four and five show us that they were enemies and not friends. As soon as they were turned down, they began to actively oppose them.

TEMPLE REBUILT, FINISH AND DEDICATED

We have already seen that the rebuilding of the temple was stopped by the opposition of the enemy. They wrote a letter to Artaxerxes which gave a false impression of Jerusalem. They called it a rebellious and bad city. The King Artaxerxes did go back in the records and find out that there had been a rebellion on the part of these people, at the very end of the kingdom (The southern kingdom of Judah). Three times they rebelled, and finally Nebuchadnezzar came and destroyed the city. But they didn't investigate thoroughly. Although they found the rebellion to be true, they did not look for the decree that had been made to rebuild the city of Jerusalem. This was a period of great discouragement. They not only stopped building; they were also tempted to walk away from the entire project. They felt that this would be the best way to solve their problems. There are many people today who think that if they just change their location everything will be excellent, and all their problems will be solved. I have been sharing with people for years the following statement, "Wherever you go, there you are". You can't walk away or run from your problems because your response is always your responsibility. This time the people did not run away. God raised up the prophets Haggai and Zechariah.

"Then the prophet Haggai and Zechariah, the son of Iddo, prophets, prophesied to the Jews who were in Judah and Jerusalem, in the name of the God of Israel, who was over them."

Ezra 5:1 NKJV

These two prophets were called by God to encourage the people to resume rebuilding the temple. They knew that there had been a decree from Cyrus, King of Persia, which granted them permission to rebuild Jerusalem. They knew it was God's will and God's time to rebuild the city. Haggai called them the "Lord's messengers. These two men were not alike. The only thing they had in common was that they were both prophets of God.

Haggai had his feet on the ground; he was a solid and stable prophet of God; he always wanted the facts. Zechariah was an entirely different type of prophet; he had tremendous visions and a message to match; he appealed to the emotions of the people, and he spoke to their hearts. These two prophets together, Haggai and Zechariah, spoke to the conscience and heart of Israel. Haggai was considered the leader, but both encouraged the people to resume their building program.

"So, Zerubbabel the son of Shealtiel, and Jeshua, the son of Jozadak, rose up and began to build the house of God, which is in Jerusalem; and the prophets of God were with them, helping them. At the same time Tattenai the governor of the region beyond the River and Shethar-Boznai and their companions came to them and spoke thus to them: "Who has commanded you to build this temple and finish this wall?""

Ezra 5:2-3 NKJV

When the work resumed, their enemies heard about it. We are told that Tatnai was a Persian governor of Samaria, and Shethar-Boznai was probably a high official. They came and challenged the workmen. Tatnai, his crowd are enemies; they were worldly men, and the Jews were not going to cast their pearls before swine. The question is, would they even understand if they said that God told them to build? The following scripture will support the previous statement.

"But the natural man does not receive the things of the Spirit of God, for they are foolishness to him; nor can he know them, because they are spiritually discerned."

I Corinthians 2:14 NKJV

"Do not answer [nor pretend to agree with the frivolous comments of] a [closed-minded] fool according to his folly, otherwise you, even you, will be like him."

Proverbs 26:4 AMP

In fact, they answered by asking a question. "Then, accordingly, we told them the names of the men who were constructing this building. In other words, we didn't see your name on the list, which was given to us. If you were part of the building crew, we would have been glad to answer you, but since your names are not on the list, we will not answer you. Basically, he was saying, "it's none of your business. You have no right to ask that question of us. "Normally the answer response that these builders gave would've put them in a very difficult situation, but notice what happens.

"But the eye of their God was upon the elders of the Jews, so that they could not make them cease till a report could go to Darius. Then a written answer was returned concerning this matter."

Ezra 5:5 NKJV

You can depend on God to keep his eye on those who are his own. So, another letter was sent to the king, by this time Darius was the king. About seven years have now gone by.

"This is a copy of the letter that Tattenai sent: The governor of the region beyond the river, and Shethar Boznai, and his companions, the Persians who were in the region beyond the river, to Darius the king. (They sent a letter to him, in which it was written thus) To Darius the king: All peace."

Ezra 5:6-7 NKJV

The preceding text now shows us the second letter the enemy sends out.

"Let it be known to the king that we went into the province of Judea, to the temple of the great God, which is being built with heavy stones, and timber is being laid in the walls; and this work goes on diligently and prospers in their hands."

Ezra 5:8 NKJV

Now, as you can see, the thought in the letter is this; We didn't go up there specifically to spy this out. We are not their enemies; we just happen to be in their neighborhood and stop by for a visit and this is what we found. The letter now concludes with this request:

"Now therefore, if it seems good to the king, let a search be made in the king's treasure house, which is there in Babylon, whether it is so that a decree was issued by King Cyrus to build this house of God at Jerusalem, and let the king send us his pleasure concerning this matter."

Ezra 5:17 NKJV

These enemies did not believe that a decree had ever been made by Cyrus; but the letter is saying that the Jews claim of such a degree is the basis on which they are rebuilding. So, they ask that a search be made. They are certain that no such decree exists, but that the people are doing this on their own.

CYRUS' DECREE CONFIRMED

A great deal has been made concerning the position and the condition of God's people. These two things are quite different, by the way. Positionally, the Jews were in the place God wanted them to be in the Land. The decree for them to return to the land was made by Cyrus, who acknowledged that he was doing it at the command of God. So, these people are in the position God wanted them to be in. However, their condition is not so good. They are discouraged. They would like to walk away from the whole business, so God raised a prophet to encourage them. It seems that God's people today tend to get their position and condition mixed up. If you are in Christ today, you are safe. Your position is good. But how is your condition? Are you a discouraged born-again believer? Are you anchored in Jesus Christ and sure of your salvation, but there are moments you might want to give up and quit? Do you want to walk away from it all?

There are many Born-Again believers that have experienced these types of moments. Why? Because even though your position is good, you might be experiencing a bad condition; this was the state of the Jews in the book of Ezra. The interesting thing is, though, that God was with his people, and His will is going to be done. Now let's look and see what happened when the enemy opened his big mouth.

"And at Achmetha, in the palace that is in the province of Media, a scroll was found, and in it a record was written thus: In the first year of King Cyrus, King Cyrus issued a decree concerning the house of God at Jerusalem: "Let the house be rebuilt, the place where they offered sacrifices; and let the foundations of it be firmly laid, its height sixty cubits and its width sixty cubits, with three rows of heavy stones and one row of new timber. Let the expenses be paid from the king's treasury. Also let the gold and silver articles of the house of God, which Nebuchadnezzar took from the temple, which is in Jerusalem and brought to Babylon. be restored, and taken back to the temple which is in Jerusalem, each to its place; and deposit them in the house of God."

Ezra 6:2-5 NKJV

As you just read in the preceding text, all of this is discovered by King Darius. Think about it, king Darius would have never known about the decree if the enemy had not mentioned it.

"Now therefore, Tattenai, governor of the region beyond the river, and Shethar-Boznai, and your companions, the Persians who are beyond the river, keep yourselves far from there. Let the work of this house of God alone; let the governor of the Jews and the elders of the Jews build this house of God on its site."

Ezra 6:6-7 NKJV

Tatnai was a governor with an important job, and he thought he could stop the building of the temple in Jerusalem. But when the decree of Cyrus was located, the present King Darius realized that it was a law of the Medes and Persians, and it could not be altered or changed; so he decided to make another decree.

"Moreover, I issue a decree as to what you shall do for the elders of these Jews, for the building of this house of God: Let the cost be paid at the king's expense from taxes on the region beyond the river; this is to be given immediately to these men, so that they are not hindered."

Ezra 6:8 NKJV

He begins by saying; Now look, not only are you to stop hindering the work, but you are also to come along side and help. You are to keep the taxes that you gathered over there on that side of the river, instead of sending them over here to Persia. You are to give the money to them for the rebuilding of the temple. The following scripture will show us how serious, he was about this decree; that he decreed a strong penalty on anyone who hindered the work.

"Also, I issue a decree that whoever alters this edict, let a timber be pulled from his house and erected, and let him be hanged on it; and let his house be made a refuse heap because of this."

Ezra 6:11 NKJV

TEMPLE FINISHED AND DEDICATED

Noticed now, that the temple is now rebuilt under the inspiration of Haggai and Zechariah.

"Then Tattenai, governor of the region beyond the River, Shethar-Boznai, and their companions diligently did according to what King Darius had sent. So, the elders of the Jews built, and they prospered through the prophesying of Haggai the prophet and Zechariah, the son of Iddo. And they built and finished it, according to the commandment of the God of Israel, and according to the command of Cyrus, Darius, and Artaxerxes king of Persia. Now the temple was finished on the third day of the month of Adar, which was in the sixth year of the reign of King Darius. Then the children of Israel, the priests and the Levites, and the rest of the descendants of the captivity, celebrated the dedication of this house of God with joy."

Ezra 6:13-16 NKJV

RETURN UNDER EZRA

Now, as we come to the second major division in the book of Ezra, the first six chapters tell us about the return of the Jews from Babylon to Jerusalem under the leadership of Zerubbabel about 50,000 Jews left Babylon at that time. The Jews had gone into Babylonian captivity because they continually turned to idolatry, and God gave them a gold cure in Babylon. Also, the Jews have disobeyed the Mosaic law in that they have not allowed the land to lie fallow (uncultivated land) every seventh year. They probably did not think it was too important. They thought they were getting by with breaking that law; but God said, "I'm going to put you out of the land for seventy years so that the land can catch up on the sabbaths it has missed. "After the land had rested and renewed itself for seventy years. God allowed his people to return. Then there was another wave of revival among the Jews who had been captives and were still living in Babylon. Ezra led a second group back to Jerusalem. Up to this point Ezra, although he is the writer of this book, is not figured in its history at all. In the final four chapters we meet the author. In chapters seven and eight we see the return of the Jews led by Ezra. In chapters nine and ten we see reformation under Ezra. Revival led to Reformation, and that is always the order. You will see this again when you study the lesson on "The Book of Nehemiah". As you study and continue to read this lesson in Ezra in the next few chapters, you're going to meet Ezra and get acquainted with him.

"Now after these things, in the reign of Artaxerxes king of Persia, Ezra the son of Seraiah, the son of Azariah, the son of Hilkiah, the son of Shallum, the son of Zadok, the son of Ahitub, the son of Amariah, the son of Azariah, the son of Meraioth, the son of Zerahiah, the son of Uzzi, the son of Bukki, the son of Abishua, the son of Phinehas, the son of Eleazar, the son of Aaron the chief priest."

Ezra 7:1-5 NKJV

Artaxerxes who gave Nehemiah permission to return to Jerusalem to rebuild the city, which marks the beginning of the great prophecy of the seventy weeks of Daniel. When you study the lesson on Nehemiah you will be hearing more about Ezra. Apparently, Ezra did not feel like returning to Jerusalem with the first delegation. There was no place for him in Jerusalem, and apparently, he was ministering to those who remained in Babylon. Now a group of about two-thousand Jews, led by Ezra, plan to go to Jerusalem. The temple had been rebuilt so that there was a place for him to minister. You're also going to find out throughout the lesson that he was also a teacher of the word of God. Phinehas, the son of Eleazar, the grandson of Aaron, is mentioned in the passage. He first appears in scripture at a time of licentious idolatry, where his zeal and action stopped the plague that was destroying Israel. Remember when Balaam the prophet was not allowed to curse Israel, he taught the king to foster intermarriage with them for the purpose of bringing the world, the flesh, and the devil into the midst of God's people. In Numbers chapter twenty-five, verses seven to eleven, it talks about how one of the Israelites took a Midianitish woman:

7 Now when Phinehas the son of Eleazar, the son of Aaron the priest, saw it, he rose from among the congregation and took a javelin in his hand; 8 and he went after the man of Israel into the tent and thrust both of them through, the man of Israel, and the woman through her body. So, the plague was stopped among the children of Israel. 9 And those who died in the plague were twenty-four thousand. 10 Then the "LORD spoke to Moses, saying: 11 "Phinehas the son of Eleazar, the son of Aaron the priest, has turned back My wrath from the children of Israel, because he was zealous with My zeal among them, so that I did not consume the children of Israel in My zeal.

Numbers 25:7-11 NKJV

When Jews married pagan people, they were drawn into the worship of their Gods. Judgment fell upon Israel in the form of a plague. Phinehas stayed the plague by executing the man who had taken the Midianitish woman and executing her also. Two lives were sacrificed to save a multitude of lives. As a reward for his efforts, God promised Phinehas that the priesthood would remain in his family forever.

"This Ezra came up from Babylon; and he was a skilled scribe in the Law of Moses, which the "LORD God of Israel had given. The king granted him all his requests, according to the hand of the "LORD God upon him."

Ezra 7:6 NKJV

Ezra was a "skilled scribe in the law of Moses. "Since he was not able to execute the office of priest, he spent his time studying the Word of God. Now he is going to be able to use what he has learned. You will find out that he is labeled "a skilled scribe" again and again. Ezra chapter seven verse twenty-one, says that Ezra had a reputation down in Babylon, even with the king, as being a scribe (teacher) of the Word of God.

"And I, even I, Artaxerxes the king, issue a decree to all the treasurers who are in the region beyond the river, that whatever Ezra the priest, the scribe of the Law of the God of heaven, may require of you, let it be done diligently,"

Ezra 7:21 NKJV

"Some of the children of Israel, the priests, the Levites, the singers, the gatekeepers, and the Nethinim, came up to Jerusalem in the seventh year of King Artaxerxes."

Ezra 7:7 NKJV

There was another revival among the Jews in Babylon, and this time about two-thousand people wanted to return to the land.

"And Ezra came to Jerusalem in the fifth month, which was in the seventh year of the king. On the first day of the first month, he began his journey from Babylon; and on the first day of the fifth month he came to Jerusalem, according to the good hand of his God upon him."

Ezra 7:8-9 NKJV

They returned to Jerusalem in the seventh year of Artaxerxes, the king. It took them almost five months to make the trip. They had no other choice but to go by foot; it was a long trip.

"For Ezra had prepared his heart to seek the Law of the "LORD, and to do it, and to teach statutes and ordinances in Israel."

Ezra 7:10 NKJV

Ezra had prepared his heart for the day that he would return to his land. He knew it was coming because he had faith in God. So, he prepared his heart and studied the law of Moses (the first five books of the Bible) and the book of Joshua, which were in existence in that day. It is the belief of many that Ezra wrote the first and second chronicles. Ezra not only studied God's word, but he also did what it said. It's one thing to study God's word and another thing to do it. Ezra also wanted to teach the word. He wanted God's people to know God's statues and judgments.

"This is a copy of the letter that King Artaxerxes gave Ezra the priest, the scribe, expert in the words of the commandments of the "LORD, and of His statutes to Israel: Artaxerxes, king of kings, To Ezra the priest, a scribe of the Law of the God of heaven: Perfect peace, and so forth. I issue a decree that all those of the people of Israel and the priests and Levites in my realm, who volunteer to go up to Jerusalem, may go with you."

Ezra 7:11-13 NKJV

Artaxerxes made a decree which allowed Ezra and his followers to return to their land. It was not a commandment that they go; but it was permission to return according to their own desires, and according to the leading of the "Lord.

"And whereas you are being sent by the king and his seven counselors to inquire concerning Judah and Jerusalem, with regard to the Law of your God which is in your hand; and whereas you are to carry the silver and gold which the king and his counselors have freely offered to the God of Israel, whose dwelling is in Jerusalem;"

Ezra 7:14-15 NKJV

Ezra had a real witness in the court because the king and his counselors made this offering to "the God of Israel," Ezra was given the authority to appoint magistrates and judges. They got together all this material. Ezra was given the King's decree; then preparation was made for them to leave. The decree reveals a tremendous reverence for God. Notice how he concludes:

"Whoever will not observe the law of your God and the law of the king, let judgment be executed speedily on him, whether it be death, or banishment, or confiscation of goods, or imprisonment.

" Ezra 7:26 NKJV

This law, of course, was in reference to the Jews after they arrived in the land. In other words, if they return to the land, they must mean business as far as their relationship to God is concerned. I want you to notice now the thanksgiving of Ezra:

"Blessed be the "LORD God of our fathers, who has put such a thing as this in the king's heart, to beautify the house of the "LORD which is in Jerusalem,"

Ezra 7:27 NKJV

Not only was the temple to be rebuilt, but it was also to be beautified. I personally think God's house should also be beautified.

"And has extended mercy to me before the king and his counselors, and before all the king's mighty princes. So, I was encouraged, as the hand of the "LORD my God was upon me; and I gathered leading men of Israel to go up with me."

Ezra 7:28 NKJV

Ezra led a great delegation back to the land. It was not as large as the first delegation, but a great amount of the leaders were in the second group. Chapter eight gives the list of Ezra's companions. Noticed that Ezra made sure that the Levites went with them. The

Nethinim, who were the servants, went along also. Then we see something that revealed how human Ezra was.

"Then I proclaimed a fast there at the river of Ahava, that we might humble ourselves before our God, to seek from Him the right way for us and our little ones and all our possessions."

Ezra 8:21 NKJV

Ezra calls for a fast and a great prayer meeting at the river of Ahava. He wanted to know God's will.

"For I was ashamed to request of the king an escort of soldiers and horsemen to help us against the enemy on the road, because we had spoken to the king, saying, "The hand of our God is upon all those for good who seek Him. but His power and His wrath are against all those who forsake Him." So, we fasted and entreated our God for this, and He answered our prayer."

Ezra 8:22-23 NKJV

He said, "You know, I went before the king and told him that the hand of our God was with us, that he will be against our enemies and will lead us back to our land. "Then Ezra looked at the delegation gathered by the river, ready to go on that long march. He looked at the families and he knew the dangers along the way. The normal thing would be to ask the king for a little help, such as a few guards to ride along with them. Then the King would say, "I thought you were trusting the "Lord.

"There are a lot of born-again believers who say that they are trusting God, but when they are facing hardship, they did it their way and not God's way. Ezra is that kind of individual when he says, "I was ashamed to go ask the king". What was the alternative? He called a prayer meeting and a fast. He said, "Oh "Lord, we just have to depend on You." You know, the "Lord puts many of us in that position many, many times.

THE RETURN TO JERUSALEM

"Then we departed from the river of Ahava on the twelfth day of the first month, to go to Jerusalem. And the hand of our God was upon us, and He delivered us from the hand of the enemy and from ambush along the road. So, we came to Jerusalem, and stayed there three days."

Ezra 8:31-32 NKJV

The king sent a great deal of gold, silver, and vessels with this delegation. This wealth was put in the care of the priests, and they needed protection, and God did watch over them, and they arrived safely at their destination. They stayed in Jerusalem for three days and took the treasure into the temple, which is the house of God.

REVIVAL UNDER EZRA

In chapter nine we come to one of the great prayers in the Bible. In three of the post captivities books there are three great ninth chapters which record prayers, which are Ezra chapter nine; Nehemiah chapter nine and Daniel chapter nine. "When these things were done, the leaders came to me, saying,

"The people of Israel and the priests and the Levites have not separated themselves from the peoples of the lands, with respect to the abominations of the Canaanites, the Hittites, the Perizzites, the Jebusites, the Ammonites, the Moabites, the Egyptians, and the Amorites."

Ezra 9:1 NKJV

The Egyptians are mentioned, and so are our other pagan peoples. The Hittites were great people, but they were heathens (people who did not acknowledge God). The people of Israel have not separated themselves from the heathen (people who did not acknowledge God). When the first delegation of the Jews returned to the land, they met with discouragement. You will learn more about this in our lesson study in the Book of Haggai (Prophecy of Haggai). We will see how he helped them overcome the discouragement that was before them. They had a lot of hurdles of discouragement, but through Haggai they could clear them. With the help of Nehemiah, who was an active layman, the walls and temple of Jerusalem were rebuilt; but there was discouragement on every hand. It has been said many times that discouragement is the devil's greatest weapon. The Jews let down their guard and intermarried with the surrounding people who did not acknowledge

God and enemies of God and Israel. That, in turn led to a practice of the abomination of the heathen (people who did not acknowledge God). The lack of separation plunges them into immorality and idolatry. People who did not acknowledge God were not in a rush to get married, because they paid little attention to the formality of marriage. Not any more than people who do not acknowledge God today.

"For they have taken some of their daughters as wives for themselves and their sons, so that the holy seed is mixed with the peoples of those lands. Indeed, the hand of the leaders and rulers has been foremost in this trespass."

Ezra 9:2 NKJV

Even the leadership was involved in this; they were even more guilty before God, why? Because privilege always increases responsibility. The return remnant (small quantity) was extremely dirty and in an unpleasant condition because of a result of poverty or neglect. Now there are several things Ezra could've done in this situation, but he didn't, so what did Ezra do?

"So, when I heard this thing, I tore my garment and my robe, and plucked out some of the hair of my head and beard and sat down astonished."

Ezra 9:3 NKJV

Remember that Ezra did not arrive in his native land until about seventy-five years after the first delegation of fifty-thousand, led by Zerubbabel. When Ezra arrived with his delegation of two thousand, he found the temple had been rebuilt, but not the walls of the city. The population was in a sad and unpleasant condition because of a result of poverty or neglect. They had intermingled and intermarried with people who did not acknowledge God. Immorality and idolatry were running unrestrained and violent. There was a lack of separation, and the Jews were in a miserable place. When all of this was brought to Ezra's attention, and he found it was accurate, he was absolutely overwhelmed and unsettled by disappointment that God's people would drop to such a low level. It would've been so easy for Ezra to point fingers at what was wrong, but he didn't. Notice what Ezra did he was so overwhelmed by the sin of his people that he "plucked off the hair of his head and beard and sat down astonish". Instead of being bitter and outspoken against them, notice the next step that Ezra took.

"Then everyone who trembled at the words of the God of Israel assembled to me, because of the transgression of those who had been carried away captive, and I sat astonished until the evening sacrifice."

Ezra 9:4 NKJV

The beginning of the proceeding scripture says, "Then everyone who trembled at the words of the God" At the date of this writing, within the last thirty-seven years that I have been saved (Born-Again) and the last thirty-two years of full-time ministry in evangelism and outreach. Sometimes I wonder, how many people really take the word of God seriously? Many people have confessed and professed to love the Word of God, hear the Word of God, but are not doers of the Word of God. They say that they believe in the Word of God, but it has no effect on them or on their lives. In Ezra 9:4 the last part of the scripture says that he "sat astonished until the evening sacrifice". Because of the transgression of those who have been carried away. I believe a lot of born-again believers today need to ask themselves a very important question; how much do I really trust and believe in the Word of God? Am I unwilling to be obedient to the Word of God? Let's look and see what Jesus said in the following scripture.

""If you love Me, keep My commandments."

John 14:15 NKJV "

At the evening sacrifice I arose from my fasting; and having torn my garment and my robe, I fell on my knees and spread out my hands to the "LORD my God."

Ezra 9:5 NKJV

What does it mean to "spread out my hands to the "LORD, my God."? It means that you are not concealing anything; it also means that when you go to God in prayer, your mind and soul stand naked before God. Ezra went to God with his hands fully extended. Ezra would not hold nothing back from God. The Apostle Paul said in his writings.

"I desire therefore that the men pray everywhere, lifting up holy hands, without wrath and doubting;"

I Timothy 2:8 NKJV

Prayer of Ezra

"And I said: "O my God, I am too ashamed and humiliated to lift my face to You, my God; for our iniquities have risen higher than our heads, and our guilt has grown up to the heavens."

Ezra 9:6 NKJV

Now I want you to notice what Ezra is saying and what he is not saying. Ezra does not say," for their iniquities are increased over their head, and their trespass is grown up into the heavens." But what he says is; for our iniquities have risen higher than our heads, and our guilt has grown up to the heavens." It is so easy to blame others why you don't go to church anymore, why you don't read your Bible, why you don't trust in the "Lord and do what he has called you to do. But it's not other peoples' sin or sins because you don't continue in the word. It is because of your own sin or sins because you don't continue to trust in God for your life. I remember when I became a born-again believer in September 1985 there's a song I used to hear in the congregation and the words are as follows "It's not my brother, not my sister, but it's me; O, "Lord, standing in the need of prayer."

"Since the days of our fathers to this day we have been very guilty, and for our iniquities we, our kings, and our priests have been delivered into the hand of the kings of the lands, to the sword, to captivity, to plunder, and to humiliation, as it is this day."

Ezra 9:7 NKJV

Ezra knew how it felt to be a captive in a foreign Land. He either had been born in captivity or had been taken captive as a young person, so he knew what it felt like. Therefore, he trembled when he recognized God would judge him. The God that we serve will always extend mercy to us. But if we were found guilty of sin, our God is a holy God; and because He is holy, He will always judge our sins.

"And now for a little while grace has been shown from the "LORD our God, to leave us a remnant to escape, and to give us a peg in His holy place, that our God may enlighten our eyes and give us a measure of revival in our."

Ezra 9:8 NKJV

Ezra said, "And now for a little while grace has been shown from the "LORD our God". The seventy years of captivity are over. God has allowed his people to return to their land, and off they go again, following people who did not acknowledge God, doing the very thing that had sent them into captivity in the first place. "There is just a remnant of us" (small quantity). Ezra was saying they were just a small quantity of us. These Jews obeyed enough to return to the land; most of the Jews did not return to the land; but those who did were small in quantity. "To give us a peg in His holy place" The King James version of the Bible uses the word "nail" instead of peg. Do you know what a "nail is"? The nail is Christ. "Your anchor is held within the veil". Why? Because you are nailed there. Jesus Christ was nailed on the cross on earth so that you and I could be nailed in heaven at the throne of God for eternity. Let's read and consider what Isaiah chapter 22:22-23, says.

"The key to the house of David I will lie on his shoulder; So, he shall open, and no one shall shut; And he shall shut, and no one shall open. I will fasten him as a peg in a secure place, and he will become a glorious throne to his father's house."

Isaiah 22:22-23 NKJV

Again, the word peg in the King James is "nail". As a born-again believer in Christ, and according to the above scripture you just read; you are nailed in a secure place, not on the cross, but in heaven for eternity. One thing about a nail, is that it is fixed and in a secure place. The Jews didn't lose their salvation, but what they lost was a great deal including the blessing of God and their reward. There are many born-again believers today that are saved and going to heaven but could lack the rewards that they could receive. Let's go back and look at a portion of the scripture in Ezra chapter nine verse eight.

"That our God may enlighten our eyes and give us a measure of revival in our bondage."

Ezra 9:38 NKJV

The above scripture shows us a true picture of revival. The word revival means "to recover life", "return to consciousness". It's referring to an individual who has a life but is now in a spiritual condition that could lead to spiritual or physical death but is revived.

"For to this end Christ died and rose and lived again, that He might be "Lord of both the dead and the living."

Romans 14:9 NKJV

When you look at the meaning of the word revival, it means that a born- again believer is in a low spiritual condition and needs to be brought back to vitality. Which is the state of being strong and active with power again. In Ezra's day you will see a real revival is going to take place as Ezra continues to pray.

"For we were slaves. Yet our God did not forsake us in our bondage; but He extended mercy to us in the sight of the kings of Persia, to revive us, to repair the house of our God, to rebuild its ruins, and to give us a wall in Judah and Jerusalem."

Ezra 9:9 NKJV

WOW...Look how good God was to the people. They confessed their sin, and God is going to bless them.

"And now, O our God, what shall we say after this? For we have forsaken Your commandments, which You commanded by Your servants the prophets, saying, 'The land which you are entering to possess is an unclean land, with the uncleanness of the peoples of the lands, with their abominations which have filled it from one end to another with their impurity. Now therefore, do not give your daughters as wives for their sons, nor take their daughters to your sons; and never seek their peace or prosperity, that you may be strong and eat the good of the land, and leave it as an inheritance to your children forever.' And after all that has come upon us for our evil deeds and for our great guilt, since You our God have punished us less than our iniquities deserve, and have given us such deliverance as this,"

Ezra 9:10-13 NKJV

In other words, Ezra is saying, "We didn't get all that was coming to us. We deserved more punishment for our sins than we received".

"Should we again break your commandments and join in marriage with the people committing these abominations? Would You not be angry with us until You had consumed us, so that there would be no remnant or survivor? O "LORD God of Israel, you are righteous. For we are left as a remnant, as it is this day. Here we are before You, in our guilt, though no one can stand before You because of this!"

Ezra 9:14-15 NKJV

Only the mercy of God, the confession of sin, the sacrifice of Christ, and the grace of God could make it possible for him to save these people, restore and revive them. God is going to do all these things because of the prayer of Ezra. The remnant (small in quantity) that was there will cry out to God for mercy. When we take that position, God is ready to hear.

REVIVAL UNDER EZRA

After this great prayer meeting, there began a movement of revival and revival always lead to reformation. What, What's reformation? Reformation means to "make changes to something with the intention of setting it back on the right path." When there is a true revival in your life, you will always experience and see effective results or genuine reformation in your life.

"Now while Ezra was praying, and while he was confessing, weeping, and bowing down before the house of God, a very large assembly of men, women, and children gathered to him from Israel; for the people wept bitterly."

Ezra 10:1 NKJV

An intense conviction of sin came over God's people and it was certainly something that was needed.

"And Shechaniah the son of Jehiel, one of the sons of Elam, spoke up and said to Ezra, "We have trespassed against our God, and have taken pagan wives from the peoples of the land; yet now there is hope in Israel despite this."

Ezra 10:2 NKJV

Shechaniah became the mouthpiece for this group of people who recognized their sin and wanted to confess. He came to Ezra and said, "We have trespassed against our God" then he continued by saying, "and have taken pagan wives from the peoples of the land". What they had done was contrary to the Law of Moses. They had not been consulted in this matter "that which was written". In other words, they had departed from the Word of God. Now he casts himself upon the mercy of God, and says, "yet now there is hope in Israel in spite of this."

"Now therefore, let us make a covenant with our God to put away all these wives and those who have been born to them, according to the advice of my master and of those who tremble at the commandment of our God; and let it be done according to the law."

Ezra 10:3 NKJV

Those who now join in confession likewise tremble at the commandment of God. That is, they not only read it and studied it; they let the Word of God have his way in their hearts. When the transgression was called to their attention, they confessed to it. They did not rationalize, excuse, or cover their sin. They came right out and confessed to it. They did this according to the Word of God.

"Arise, for this matter is your responsibility. We also are with you. Be of good courage and do it." Then Ezra arose, and made the leaders of the priests, the Levites, and all Israel swear an oath that they would do according to this word. So, they swore an oath. Then Ezra rose from before the house of God and went into the chamber of Jehohanan, the son of Eliashib; and when he came there, he ate no bread and drank no water; for he mourned because of the guilt of those from the captivity."

Ezra 10:4-6 NKJV

Breaking the law of God was a very serious thing. They were before him with great prevail, a soul. What everyone went through was rather heart-breaking; but, but the word of God had been transgressed, and the people had to repent. Revival starts when we begin to follow God. The word of God will always bring conviction to your heart. Whenever you go to God with a confession, there is always a repentance, and the results will always be a strengthening of improvement in your life. Instead of first preaching repentance to unbelievers, it might be a great idea just to share with others, to believe in Jesus and let repentance follow.

"So, they said, "Believe on the "Lord Jesus Christ, and you will be saved, you and your household."

Acts 16:31 NKJV

When an individual comes to Christ as Savior, something else happens, just like it did in first Thessalonians chapter one, verse nine Paul said.

"For they themselves declare concerning us what manner of entry we had to you, and how you turned to God from idols to serve the living and true God,"

I Thessalonians 1:9 NKJV

"Turning to God" took priority over "turning to idols." Repentance does not precede Faith. Faith goes before, and repentance follows, just like night-time will follow daytime. If repentance does not follow faith, the faith is not genuine, it isn't saving faith. Repentance could be possibly the thing that is lacking in most churches. Have you ever noticed that in the Bible, God asks the church to repent? In the seven letters to the seven churches of Asia Minor, recorded in the book of revelation, God asked all but two of them to repent. God was talking to believers, not to unbelievers.

THE LOVELESS CHURCH

"To the angel of the church of Ephesus write, 'These things says He who holds the seven stars in His right hand, who walks in the midst of the seven golden lamp stands: "I know your works, your labor, your patience, and that you cannot bear those who are evil. And you have tested those who say they are apostles and are not, and have found them liars; and you have persevered and have patience, and have labored for My name's sake, and have not become weary. Nevertheless, I have this against you, that you have left your first love. Remember therefore, from where you have fallen; repent and do the first works; or else I will come to you quickly and remove your lampstand from its place—unless you repent. But this you have, that you hate the deeds of the Nicolaitans, which I also hate. "He who has an ear, let him hear what the Spirit says to the churches. To him who overcomes I will give to eat from the tree of life, which is in the midst of the Paradise of God."

Revelation 2:1-7 NKJV

THE PERSECUTED CHURCH

"And to the angel of the church in Smyrna write, 'These things says the First and the Last, who was dead, and came to life: "I know your works, tribulation, and poverty (but you are rich); and I know the blasphemy of those who say they are Jews, and are not, but are a synagogue of Satan. Do not fear any of those things which you are about to suffer. Indeed, the devil is about to throw some of you into prison, that you may be tested, and you will have tribulation ten days. Be faithful until death, and I will give you the crown of life. "He who has an ear, let him hear what the Spirit says to the churches. He who overcomes shall not be hurt by the second death."

Revelation 2:8-11 NKJV

THE COMPROMISING CHURCH

"And to the angel of the church in Pergamos write, 'These things says He who has the sharp two-edged sword: "I know your works, and where you dwell, and where Satan's throne is. And you hold fast to My name, and did not deny My faith, even in the days in which Antipas was My faithful martyr, who was killed among you, where Satan dwells. But I have a few things against you, because you have those who hold the doctrine of Balaam, who taught Balak to put a stumbling block before the children of Israel; to eat things sacrificed to idols, and to commit sexual immorality. Thus, you also have those who hold the doctrine of the Nicolaitans, which thing I hate. Repent, or else I will come to you quickly, and will fight against them with the sword of My mouth. "He who has an ear, let him hear what the Spirit says to the churches. To him who overcomes I will give some of the hidden manna to eat. And I will give him a white stone, and on the stone a new name written which no one knows except him who receives it".

Revelation 2:12-17 NKJV

THE CORRUPT CHURCH

"And to the angel of the church in Thyatira write, 'These things says the Son of God, who has eyes like a flame of fire, and His feet like fine brass: "I know your works, love, service, faith, and your patience; and as for your works, the last are more than the first. Nevertheless, I have a few things against you, because you allow that woman Jezebel, who calls herself a prophetess, to teach and seduce My servants to commit sexual immorality and eat things sacrificed to idols. And I gave her time to repent of her sexual immorality, and she did not repent. Indeed, I will cast her into a sickbed, and those who commit adultery with her into great tribulation, unless they repent of their deeds. I will kill her children with death, and all the churches shall know that I am He who searches the minds and hearts. And I will give to each one of you according to your works. "Now to you I say, and to the rest in Thyatira, as many as do not have this doctrine, who have not known the depths of Satan, as they say, I will put on you no other burden. But hold fast what you have till I come. And he who overcomes, and keeps My works until the end, to him I will give power over the nations— 'He shall rule them with a rod of iron; They shall be dashed to pieces like the potters' vessels — as I also have received from My Father; and I will give him the morning star. "He who has an ear, let him hear what the Spirit says to the churches."

Revelation 2:18-29 NKJV

THE DEAD CHURCH

""And to the angel of the church in Sardis write, 'These things say He who has the seven Spirits of God and the seven stars: "I know your works, that you have a name that you are alive, but you are dead. Be watchful, and strengthen the things which remain, that are ready to die, for I have not found your works perfect before

God. Remember therefore how you have received and heard; hold fast and repent. Therefore, if you will not watch, I will come upon you as a thief, and you will not know what hour I will come upon you. You have a few names even in Sardis who have not defiled their garments; and they shall walk with Me in white, for they are worthy. He who overcomes shall be clothed in white garments, and I will not blot out his name from the Book of Life; but I will confess his name before My Father and before His angels. "He who has an ear, let him hear what the Spirit says to the churches."

Revelation 3:1-6 NKJV

THE FAITHFUL CHURCH

"And to the angel of the church in Philadelphia write, 'These things say He who is holy, He who is true, "He who has the key of David. He who opens, and no one shuts, and shuts, and no one opens": "I know your works. See, I have set before you an open door, and no one can shut it; for you have a little strength, have kept My word, and have not denied My name. Indeed, I will make those of the synagogue of Satan, who say they are Jews and are not, but lie—indeed I will make them come and worship before your feet, and to know that I have loved you. Because you have kept My command to persevere, I also will keep you from the hour of trial which shall come upon the whole world, to test those who dwell on the earth. Behold, I am coming quickly! Hold fast what you have, that no one may take your crown. He who overcomes, I will make him a pillar in the temple of My

God, and he shall go out no more. I will write on him the name of My God and the name of the city of My God, the New Jerusalem, which comes down out of heaven from My God. And I will write on him My new name. "He who has an ear, let him hear what the Spirit says to the churches."

Revelation 3:7-13 NKJV

THE LUKEWARM CHURCH

"And to the angel of the church of the Laodiceans write, 'These things says the Amen, the Faithful and True Witness, the Beginning of the creation of God: "I know your works, that you are neither cold nor hot. I could wish you were cold or hot. So then, because you are lukewarm, and neither cold nor hot, I will vomit you out of My mouth. Because you say, 'I am rich, have become wealthy, and have need of nothing'—and do not know that you are wretched, miserable, poor, blind, and naked— I counsel you to buy from Me gold refined in the fire, that you may be rich; and white garments; that you may be clothed, that the shame of your nakedness may not be revealed; and anoint your eyes with eye salve, that you may see. As much as I love, I rebuke and chasten. Therefore, be zealous and repent. Behold, I stand at the door and knock. If anyone hears My voice and opens the door, I will come into him and dine with him, and he with Me. To him who overcomes I will grant to sit with Me on My throne, as I also overcame and sat down with My Father on His throne. "He who has an ear, let him hear what the Spirit says to the churches."

Revelation 3:14-22 NKJV

God is saying to his church, "Repent, come back to Me. I feel one of the greatest things that we need today is a revival, and a revival will not come without repentance among born-again believers. In Ezra's day, God's people were no longer indifferent in the church. Ezra went to God in genuine repentance, and others are following his example.

"And they issued a proclamation throughout Judah and Jerusalem to all the descendants of the captivity, that they must gather at Jerusalem, and that whoever would not come within three days, according to the instructions of the leaders and elders, all his property would be confiscated, and he himself would be separated from the assembly of those from the captivity."

Ezra 10:7-8 NKJV

We can see now how they were making a real line of separation. They are under the Mosaic Law and are removing all the chaff that they can from the good wheat. It would take about three days to come from any section of that land, and this proclamation was directed to all those who had come out of Babylonian captivity, who had returned to rebuild the city, the walls, and the temple. They were to come together for a time of spiritual refreshing, but repentance should follow. Those who would not come because they felt that things were not being done the way they wanted them done, or had some other objection, were to be cast out of the congregation. It only takes a few unhappy and complaining people in a local church to disrupt a spiritual movement. God doesn't want you to be bitter. He wants you to be better. Why? Because the root of bitterness has destroyed a lot of people throughout the body of Christ. Read the following scripture.

"Looking carefully lest anyone fall short of the grace of God; lest any root of bitterness springing up cause trouble, and by this many become defiled."

Hebrews 12:15 NKJV

Let's continue with our lesson. "So, all the men of Judah and Benjamin gathered in Jerusalem within three days. It was the ninth month, on the twentieth of the month; and all the people sat in the open square of the house of God, trembling because of this matter and because of heavy rain. Then Ezra the priest, stood up and said to them.

"You have transgressed and have taken pagan wives, adding to the guilt of Israel. Now therefore, make confession to the LORD God of your fathers, and do His will; separate yourselves from the peoples of the land, and from the pagan wives."

Ezra 10:9-11 NKJV

According to the following scripture it says.

"But prove yourselves doers of the word [actively and continually obeying God's precepts], and not merely listeners [who hear the word but fail to internalize its meaning], deluding yourselves [by unsound reasoning contrary to the truth]."

James 1:22 AMP

CHAPTER 2

THE BOOK OF HAGGAI

With the Babylonian exile in the past, and a newly returned group of Jews back in the land, the work of rebuilding the temple begins. However, sixteen years after the process began, the people have not finished the project; for their personal affairs have interfered with God's business. Haggai preaches an effective message that stirred up the nation to finish the temple. He calls the builders to renewed courage, holiness of life, and renewed faith in God. Haggai was a prophet to restore the remnant who returned to Jerusalem after the seventy-year captivity. Haggai and Zechariah prophesied during the same period, but their approach was different. They both challenged and encouraged the returned remnant to re-build the temple and then to rebuild the walls of Jerusalem.

"Then the prophet Haggai and Zechariah the son of Iddo, prophets, prophesied to the Jews who were in Judah and Jerusalem, in the name of the God of Israel, who was over them. So, Zerubbabel the son of Shealtiel and Jeshua the son of Jozadak rose up and began to build the house of God which is in Jerusalem; and the prophets of God were with them, helping them."

Ezra 5:1-2 NKJV

Haggai and Zechariah are mentioned in this historical book of Ezra as the two prophets who encouraged the people to rebuild the temple and aided them in it.

"So, the elders of the Jews built, and they prospered through the prophesying of Haggai the prophet and Zechariah the son of Iddo. They built and finished it, according to the commandment of the God of Israel, and according to the command of Cyrus, Darius, and Artaxerxes king of Persia."

Ezra 6:14 NKJV

"In the second year of King Darius, in the sixth month, on the first day of the month, the word of the "LORD came by Haggai the prophet to Zerubbabel the son of Shealtiel, governor of Judah, and to Joshua the son of Jehozadak, the high priest, saying,"

Haggai 1:1 NKJV

"And they will fall by the edge of the sword and be led away captive into all nations. And Jerusalem will be trampled by Gentiles until the times of the Gentiles are fulfilled."

Luke 21:24 NKJV

As you and study this book, you will see how Haggai repeatedly refers to the Word of the "Lord. He is making it clear that he is not speaking his own thoughts but is giving the Word of God to his people. Part of the preceding scripture of Haggai chapter one verse one says, "To Zerubbabel, the son of Shealtiel, governor of Judah". The name Zerubbabel means "sown in Babylon" which means he was born in captivity down in Babylon. He was in the line of David, the grandson of Jehoiachin.

"The sons of Jehoiakim were Jeconiah his son and Zedekiah his son. And the sons of Jeconiah were Assir, Shealtiel his son, and Malchiram, Pedaiah, Shenazzar, Jecamiah, Hoshama, and Nedabiah. The sons of Pedaiah were Zerubbabel and Shimei. The sons of Zerubbabel were Meshullam, Hananiah, Shelomith their sister,"

I Chronicles 3:16-19 NKJV

Cyrus appointed Zerubbabel to be governor of Judah.

"Jehozadak went into captivity when the "LORD carried Judah and Jerusalem into captivity by the hand of Nebuchadnezzar."

I Chronicles 6:15 NKJV

When the Israelites returned from Babylonian captivity to their own land, they returned with great anticipation, and their enthusiasm for rebuilding ran high. But they met gigantic obstacles which required strong efforts and hardships. After they had gone through a hardship, they became very discouraged when they began to build the temple. The difficulties seemed impossible. So, they rationalized and decided that it was not the time to build. In other words, this was their relief. They wanted to remain comfortable.

Thus speaks the LORD of hosts, saying, "This people says, "The time has not come, the time that the "LORD's house should be built."

Haggai 1:2 NKJV

They said, "It is so hard, evidently God doesn't intend for us to build the temple." They had laid the foundations of the temple, but the opposition of the Samaritans was so intense that they stopped building. Their excuse was, "The time has not come, the time that the, Lord's house should be built hasn't come yet". When you read the Book of Nehemiah, you will see that, when they were building the walls of Jerusalem, the opposition was great. In other words, it intensified. Just like in the Book of Nehemiah, they had the same type of opposition, that intensity in the Book of Ezra when rebuilding the temple. The verse shows that unlike other times when God would say "My people" in this context, He didn't. This does not mean that God disowned them, but that He was displeased with them. They were not in His will, and covered their disobedience with excuses saying "The time has not come, the time that the "LORD's house should be built.

Then the word of the LORD came by Haggai the prophet, saying, "Is it time for you yourselves to dwell in your paneled houses, and this temple to lie in ruins?"

Haggai 1:3-4 NKJV

They said it was time to build the "Lord's house, but they had time to build their own houses. The "Lord pointed out that their houses were paneled houses, which meant that the homes were beautiful and built well. During the fifteen years while they were building their homes, as stated earlier, the "Lord's house was not being built. At the current time of the writing of this book I have been serving in full-time ministry for over thirty-one years. Many people throughout the years have contacted our ministry and ask about serving the city with excellence through evangelism and outreach. My office always gives the same answer. "There is a commitment to the cause." They continue to make statements like, "I feel that God wants me to do something difference" or "I don't have the time anymore to help". Most people give up and quit what God has called them to do because of difficulty; instead of being like a postage stamp, sticking with their assignment, they have been given. It's vitally important to stay on the path that God has laid out for you until you get to your destination.

"And let us not grow weary while doing good, for in due season we shall reap if we do not lose heart."

Galatians 6:9 NKJV

Most people will stay consistent with a task, usually if it benefits them only. They will make the effort to accomplish that which will always be to their advantage. In the book of Haggai my question is, how were the people able to build their own home without difficulties, but they were not willing to face the same difficulties to build the "Lord's house. The only excuse they had, and I repeat, "The time has not come, the time that the "LORD's house should be built." Just because something is difficult and hard does not mean that it's not the "Lords will. Remember, if there were no oppositions then everybody will do it. Let me ask you two questions, "How much time are you spending on yourself and how much are you doing for God? Are you trying to fit God into your schedule or are you trying to fit your schedule into God? Most people have an "EGO PROBLEM", They are always "Edging God Out" instead of "Edging God In", Again. The Israelites said it was not the time for God's house to be built; but God is saying, how then can you build your house? If you pay attention and listen really closely when most people are talking, you will find out that what they do for themselves is more than what they are doing for God. The following scripture makes it very clear on how we should live our lives.

"Let each of you look out not only for his own interests but also for the interests of others."

Philippians 2:4 NKJV

2 1-4 If you've gotten anything at all out of following Christ, if his love has made any difference in your life, if being in a community of the Spirit means anything to you, if you have a heart, if you care—then do me a favor: Agree with each other, love each other, be deep-spirited friends. Don't push your way to the front; don't sweet-talk your way to the top. Put yourself aside, and help others get ahead. Don't be obsessed with getting your own advantage. Forget yourselves long enough to lend a helping hand.

Philippians 2:1- 4 MSG.

"Now therefore, thus says the "LORD of hosts: "Consider your ways!"

Haggai 1:5 NKJV

God is now calling their attention to something that is very practical. He says, "consider your ways," in other words, he was saying, do a self-examination of yourself and look what is happening to you.

"You have sown much, and bring in little; You eat, but do not have enough; You drink, but you are not filled with drink; You clothe yourselves, but no one is warm; And he who earns wages, earns wages to put into a bag with holes." Thus, says the "LORD of hosts, "consider your ways!"

Haggai 1:6-7 NKJV

God was judging them concerning their material things, and they were not recognizing it as his judgment.

"If you endure chastening, God deals with you as with sons; for what son is there whom a father does not chasten?"

Hebrews 12:7 NKJV

Remember that whenever God disciplines you, there is always a reason for it. It is always good for you, as a born-again believer in Christ, to consider your ways in everything you do. You need to examine your heart to see why God is allowing you to go through your situation. For the people of Israel there had been crop failure, famine, little money to buy clothes or food, and they had no savings account. But they never once to responsibility for their own actions and disobedience; they tried to explain it in other ways. Difficulties always come to you for a purpose. God will not let anything happen to you unless it's for a purpose. He uses difficult situations to develop your character and a pure heart in life. That is why God said, "consider your ways."

For the "LORD knows the way of the righteous, but the way of the ungodly shall perish."

Psalms 1:6 NKJV

"Good understanding gains favor, But the way of the unfaithful is hard."

Proverbs 13:15 NKJV

"There is a way that seems right to a man, but its end is the way of death."

Proverbs 14:12 NKJV

"All we like sheep have gone astray; We have turned, everyone, to his own way; And the "LORD has laid on Him the iniquity of us all."

Isaiah 53:6 NKJV

"Let the wicked forsake his way, And the unrighteous man his thoughts; Let him return to the "LORD, And He will have mercy on him; And to our God, For He will abundantly pardon."

Isaiah 55:7 NKJV

""For as the heavens are higher than the earth, so are My ways higher than your ways. And My thoughts than your thoughts."

Isaiah 55:9 NKJV

"Thus says the "LORD: "Stand in the ways and see, and ask for the old paths, where the good way is, and walk in it; Then you will find rest for your souls. But they said, 'We will not walk in it.'"

Jeremiah 6:16 NKJV

"O LORD, I know the way of man is not in himself; It is not in man who walks to direct his own steps."

Jeremiah 10:23 NKJV

"Your ears shall hear a word behind you, saying, this is the way, walk in it.Whenever you turn to the right hand or whenever you turn to the left."

Isaiah 30:21 NKJV

"Most assuredly, I say to you, he who does not enter the sheepfold by the door, but climbs up some other way, the same is a thief and a robber. But he who enters by the door is the shepherd of the sheep."

John 10:1-2 NKJV

"I am the door. If anyone enters by Me, he will be saved, and will go in and out and find pasture."

John 10:9 NKJV

What God is saying to his people in the preceding scriptures, he wants them to consider their ways. God began to give them the solution to their problems. He gives them a command to build the temple, and he gives them three things that they are to do. The children of Israel had a conflict of interests. They had put their own homes before God's house. Jesus said in the sermon on the mount

"But seek first the kingdom of God and His righteousness, and all these things shall be added to you."

Matthew 6:33 NKJV

As a believer in Jesus, you, already have everything you need. Materials possessions are not bad because I believe God wants his children to live a life where every need is met. Let's look at John chapter 10:10 in the amplified version.

"The thief comes only in order to steal and kill and destroy. I came that they may have and enjoy life, and have it in abundance [to the full, till it overflows]."

John 10:10 AMP

The things that many people have today are not wrong, but it is wrong when the things that they have supersede the God that you are supposed to be serving. It's vitally important to always remember that God is the one that shall be praised and honored, not stuff. For over thirty-one years I have consistently shared with people to not praise and honor the creation more than the creator that gave you the things to enjoy life. The following scripture shows us that God does not have a problem with you having things.

"But first and most importantly, seek (aim at, strive after) His kingdom and His righteousness [His way of doing and being right—the attitude and character of God], and all these things will be given to you as well."

Matthew 6:33 AMP

He just doesn't want things to have you! At all the funeral services I have directed and seen, I still have not noticed a U-Haul following the limousines to the cemetery. In the next verse, God tells the people in Haggai's day what they are to do:

"Go up to the mountains and bring wood and build the temple, that I may take pleasure in it and be glorified," says the "LORD."

Haggai 1:8 NKJV

God told them to do three things:

Go up to the mountain

Bring Wood

Build the temple

If you are not ready to go to work and do what God wants you to do, whatever that might be. God believes in work, and the message of the book of Haggai is about work.

"But be doers of the word, and not hearers only, deceiving yourselves."

James 1:22 NKJV

The reason they had not built the temple was that they were just lazy. They continue to make the excuse that, "The time isn't right, it's not the will of God to build at this time". The people had made excuses because of bad circumstances, but God said that they needed to "considered their ways", and now he tells them to get to work and start building the temple. Through- out my years of ministry I have noticed that there are a lot of people that expect people to do the work that God has given them to do but God did not tell them to do what he has called you to do. There are many people sitting on the sideline today being a spectator instead of a participator. I believe there are at least five groups of people that exist today.

1. COMMENTATOR-This individual always asks, "what happened", they rarely show up at church or community events, such as Sunday school weekly services, prayer community outreaches and when they finally show up to something they don't get involved and work, but they are good at talking.

2. SPECTATOR-This individual always "watch things happen", they always see problems throughout the community but never provide an answer for the problem.

3. NON-PARTICIPATOR -This individual "always let things happen", they are physically at community meetings but are mentally thinking about something else.

4. IRRITATOR -This individual represents all of the above. They are always frustrating everyone, and they are a huge liability instead of an asset.

5. PARTICIPATOR -This individual "makes things happen", these are the type of people that will get the job done

CHAPTER 3

NEHEMIAH

Nehemiah, contemporary of Ezra and cupbearer to the king in Persian Palace, leads the third and last return to Jerusalem after the Babylonian exile. His concern for the welfare of Jerusalem and its inhabitants prompts him to take bold action. Granted permission to return to his homeland, Nehemiah challenges his countrymen. The key verses for the book of Nehemiah are as follows.

"So it was, when I heard these words, that I sat down and wept, and mourned for many days; I was fasting and praying before the God of heaven."

Nehemiah 1:4 NKJV

"So, I sent messengers to them, saying, "I am doing a great work, so that I cannot come down. Why should the work cease while I leave it and go down to you?""

Nehemiah 6:3 NKJV

Originally Ezra and Nehemiah were one book known as the 'Book of Ezra'. Later a division was made, and the two sections became distinguished as the first and the second books of Ezra. Eventually the second book was called the book of "Nehemiah". The book of Nehemiah begins with Nehemiah receiving the word that Jerusalem needs help, both physically and spiritually. Nehemiah becomes heart broken and weeps for many days. Nehemiah was the cupbearer for Artaxerxes, the king of Persia, and was granted permission to return to Jerusalem to rebuild the walls of the city and is made governor. Nehemiah so inspired the people that they gave a lot of money, supplies, and manpower to complete the wall in fifty-two days through opposition. Nehemiah had a "Goal" which was to "Rebuild" the walls of Jerusalem, and nothing less than total completion would be satisfactory. I believe that all believers in Christ need to have goals in life that include God goals that reflect vision and goals that really matter. As believers in Christ, we are supposed to have genuine compassion for others who have physical and/or spiritual hurt.

The words of Nehemiah the son of Hachaliah. It came to pass in the month of Chislev, in the twentieth year, as I was in Shushan, the citadel, that Hanani one of my brethren, came with men from Judah; and I asked them concerning the Jews who had escaped, who had survived the captivity, and concerning Jerusalem. And they said to me, "The survivors who are left from the captivity in the province are there in great distress and reproach. The wall of Jerusalem is also broken down, and its gates are burned with fire."

Nehemiah 1:1-3 NKJV

The words of Nehemiah the son of Hachaliah. It came to pass in the month of Chislev, in the twentieth year, as I was in Shushan, the citadel, that Hanani one of my brethren, came with men from Judah; and I asked them concerning the Jews who had escaped, who had survived the captivity, and concerning Jerusalem. And they said to me, "The survivors who are left from the captivity in the province are there in great distress and reproach. The wall of Jerusalem is also broken down, and its gates are burned with fire." "In Shushan the citadel": Nehemiah lived in Shushan, the capital city of the Persians; and he lived in the citadel–that is, the fortified palace of the Persians. Right away, we know Nehemiah is someone important, living in the king's palace of Persia. Nehemiah's body was in Persia, but his heart and his interest were in Jerusalem, which was eight-hundred miles away. He wanted to know from those returning how the people and the city were doing. Nehemiah had more important things to think about than a distant city he had never been to, and a people he had never met. But because his heart was for the things of God, his heart was not on himself, but on others. Nehemiah had the heart of

If I forget you, O Jerusalem, let my right hand forget its skill! If I do not remember you, let my tongue cling to the roof of my mouth, if I do not exalt Jerusalem above my chief joy.

Psalms 137:5-6 NKJV

If Jerusalem was special to God, then it would also be special to Nehemiah. The news he received was not encouraging. The people were called survivors; this was not a hopefulness title. They were in great distress and reproach; and the walls of the city itself were broken down, and the city gates were burned with fire. The condition of the people and the city walls were connected. In the ancient world, a city without walls was a city completely open and vulnerable to its enemies. They had no defense, no protection at all. An un-walled city was always a backwater town, with nothing valuable in it. If there was anything of value in an un-walled city, it could be stolen away easily because there was no one to stop it. Those living in an un-walled city lived in constant stress and tension; they never knew when they might be attacked. Every man lived in constant fear for his wife and children. The temple could be rebuilt, but never made beautiful, because anything valuable would be taken easily. No wonder the people lived in constant distress living only as survivors. Gods plan for you is to live not only as a survivor, but he wants you to be a conqueror.

"Yet in all these things we are more than conquerors and gain an overwhelming victory through Him who loved us, so much that He died for us. For I am convinced [and continue to be convinced—beyond any doubt] that neither death, nor life, nor angels, nor principalities, nor things present and threatening, nor things to come, nor powers."

Romans 8:37-38 AMP

"So, what do you think? With God on our side like this, how can we lose? If God didn't hesitate to put everything on the line for us, embracing our condition and exposing himself to the worst by sending his own Son, is there anything else he wouldn't gladly and freely do for us? And who would dare tangle with God by messing with one of God's chosen? Who would dare even to point a finger? The One who died for us—who was raised to life for us! — is in the presence of God at this very moment sticking up for us. Do you think anyone is going to drive a wedge between us and Christ's love for us? There is no way! Not trouble, not hard times, not hatred, not hunger, not homelessness, not bullying threats, not backstabbing, not even the worst sins listed in Scripture: They kill us in cold blood because they hate you. We're sitting ducks; they pick us off one by one. None of this fazes us because Jesus loves us. I'm absolutely convinced that nothing—nothing living or dead, angelic or demonic, today or tomorrow, high or low, thinkable or unthinkable—absolutely nothing can get between us and God's love because of the way that Jesus our Master has embraced us."

Romans 8:31-39 MSG

"So it was, when I heard these words, that I sat down and wept, and mourned for many days; I was fasting and praying before the God of heaven."

Nehemiah 1:4 NKJV

Nehemiah's immediate reaction caused him to have no strength in his legs because the text says, he sat down and began to weep and mourn. God was going to use Nehemiah to do something great about the situation. But first, God had to do something in Nehemiah. Whenever God calls and gives you an assignment to do a great work in your community, city, state or around the world, He first starts by doing a great work in you. God was preparing Nehemiah's' heart about the welfare of the people in Jerusalem while he was actively serving in his position in Persia. God saw the need from heaven, but nothing could be done until the right man also felt the need on earth. God accomplished the need through Nehemiah. Nehemiah couldn't do this alone. He had to be a leader one who influences other people to get the job done. Nehemiah is a book all about leadership something we obviously need today. Since leadership is influence, leadership applies to everyone. Everyone has an area of leadership. In some way, everyone is a leader; the question is if they are a good leader or a bad leader. A true Leader has to prepare themselves for the assignment that has been given to them because there is no "opportunity without an opposition". Nehemiah's reaction went beyond an immediate emotion. For many people a concern for something or someone will come and then quickly pass. But if it is from the "Lord the burden will remain until the problem that prompted the burden is solved. Always remember that Jesus is the answer that solves every problem. Notice what Nehemiah didn't do; he didn't complain or see who could fix this problem. He immediately did what he knew he could which was to pray and seek God in this situation. Nehemiah also had a clear understanding of Whom he fasted and prayed to. There are many "Gods" people trust in, but there's only one "God" who can really meet your needs.

"And my God will liberally supply (fill until full) your every need according to His riches in glory in Christ Jesus."

Philippians 4:19 AMP

"And I said: "I pray, "LORD God of heaven, O great and awesome God, You who keep Your covenant and mercy with those who love You and observe Your commandments, please let Your ear be attentive and Your eyes open, that You may hear the prayer of Your servant which I pray before You now, day and night, for the children of Israel Your servants, and confess the sins of the children of Israel which we have sinned against You. Both my father's house and I have sinned. We have acted very corruptly against You, and have not kept the commandments, the statutes, nor the ordinances which You commanded Your servant, Moses."

Nehemiah 1:5-7 NKJV

Prayer is always essential to leadership. It's very important to know when you have a vision from God. Following are three questions I want to ask you regarding if you have a vision from God.

1.Is it BIGGER THAN YOU?

2.If you CAN'T STOP THINKING ABOUT IT?

3.WHAT ARE YOU WILLING TO GIVE UP!

When your vision is so big that only God can accomplish it, then you obviously must pray. If prayer isn't necessary to accomplish your vision, your vision isn't big enough. Remember, there is a difference between a GOOD IDEA and a GOD IDEA. You see, good ideas might come to pass, but God's ideas will come to pass. There are many people who think achievements and accomplishments are the same, but they are different. Achievements are when you set goals to achieve toward the accomplishments. Accomplishments are when all the goals have been completed resulting in goals accomplishment and assignment, task or Job completed. Nehemiah prayed for four months before he did anything. Later, when the work of rebuilding the walls began, it only took 52 days to finish the job. But that 52-day project had a "four-month foundation of prayer". Nehemiah took his pain and stress to God in prayer and was able to leave it there. Prayer will relieve your stress and will give you strength; when you wait on the "Lord in prayer; He will renew your strength.

"But those who wait for the "LORD [who expect, look for, and hope in Him] Will gain new strength and renew their power; They will lift up their wings [and rise up close to God] like eagles [rising toward the sun]; They will run and not become weary, they will walk and not grow tired."

Isaiah 40:31 AMP

Nehemiah's humility begins by understanding that there is a God in the heavens and I'm not him! Nehemiah's' humility also led him to his complete dependence on God. Nehemiah desperately asked God to hear the prayer of Your servant. Nehemiah's total dependence was on God. Only God could help, and if God would only hear, Nehemiah knew, He would help. Nehemiah humility plainly and simply confessed sin, without any attempt at excusing the sin. We must always avoid excusing ourselves in the confession of our sin. May we never say, ""Lord, if I sinned" or ""Lord, I'm sorry. You will always find freedom in open, honest confession, without any attempt at excuse or wondering "if" you sinned or not. Nehemiah was a Godly man; but he openly and passionately put himself in his father's house and prayed by using "we" instead of "they."

"Remember, I pray, the word that You commanded Your servant Moses, saying, ' If you are unfaithful, I will scatter you among the nations; but if you return to Me, and keep My commandments and do them, though some of you were cast out to the farthest part of the heavens, yet I will gather them from there, and bring them to the place which I have chosen as a dwelling for My name.' Now these are Your servants and Your people, whom You have redeemed by Your great power, and by Your strong hand."

Nehemiah 1:8- 10 NKJV

This is a powerful way to come to God, asking Him to remember His promises. Nehemiah said,

"LORD, you made a promise to Moses and this nation, I ask you now to make good on it." Nehemiah quoted from both Leviticus 26 and Deuteronomy 30. This, no doubt, is the secret to the power of prayer: to plead for the promises of God. Have any of your children ever come to you said "Daddy or Mommy, you promised"; I want to realize that your God in heaven delights in keeping his promises as you open your mouth to pray. Let's read what God says in the following scripture.

"I am the LORD your God, who brought you out of the land of Egypt; Open your mouth wide, and I will fill it."

Psalms 81:10 NKJV

God will not open His storehouse until you open your mouth in asking Him to perform His promises. Nehemiah quoted a conditional promise. The condition was returning to God and keeping His commandments. He really couldn't know if the nation was keeping the commandments, but he knew that he was keeping them, and because he had identified himself with the nation in their sin the nation could also identify itself with Nehemiah in his Godly fulfillment of these conditions.

"O "Lord, I pray, please let Your ear be attentive to the prayer of Your servant, and to the prayer of Your servants who desire to fear Your name; and let Your servant prosper this day, I pray, and grant him mercy in the sight of this man." For I was the king's cupbearer."

Nehemiah 1:11 NKJV

Nehemiah concluded by asking God to bless him when he speaks to the king of Persia about the matter. Nehemiah was going to do something about the walls of Jerusalem and the people, and he knew without God's help he could do nothing.

"I can do all things [which He has called me to do] through Him who strengthens and empowers me [to fulfill His purpose—I am self-sufficient in Christ's sufficiency; I am ready for anything and equal to anything through Him who infuses me with inner strength and confident peace.]"

Philippians 4:13 AMP

When Nehemiah asked the question, "Let your servant prosper this day" it was a prayer of a man of action. Nehemiah's prayer was not "God, make it all better" or "God, get somebody else to do it. Instead, his prayer was "God, use me to make it better." Nehemiah did not wait to see what other people would do, but he wanted to do something himself." Nehemiah occupied the office of the royal cupbearer, which was a place of great honor in the Persian court. Nehemiah was daily in the presence of the King, and was able to see how he was in different seasons of life, and had favor with the king in certain requests where others were denied. Cupbearers were generally eunuchs. They were often found represented on Assyrian monuments, holding the cup in the left hand and a fly-flap made of split palm leaves in the right hand. A long napkin that was embroidered and fringed, was thrown over the left shoulder for the king to wipe his lips with. Three men played important roles in the rebuilding of Jerusalem:

- Zerubbabel, the prince, who represents the political side.
- Ezra the priest
- Nehemiah the layman

Since the king, priest, and the prophet failed to rebuild the walls of Jerusalem, God raised up a layman named Nehemiah. You might be wondering, what is a layman? A layman is a non-ordained member of the church. In other words, Nehemiah was a congregational member who was responsible for rebuilding the walls of Jerusalem. Nehemiah believed in watching and working. He also believes in working and praying. Even though Nehemiah had a good government job in Persia, he was also a cupbearer to the king and was an honest man! He could have remained in Persia, and even though he had a very important position, he still had a concern for the work of God. Have you ever allowed your position to dictate what you are supposed to do for God? Have you tried to fit God into your schedule instead of fitting your schedule into God? This congregational member named Nehemiah, had become extremely concerned about the report that he was given regarding the captivity of the people. Nehemiah could have started making excuses like most people did and say: "They deserved it and they got what they had coming to them" "Oh, I am so sorry to hear that" "I'll put you on my prayer list" "God bless you" "I'll be lifting you up" "That's not my problem" In the book of Ezra even he had a reaction to the condition of the people as a priest. He was concerned, now as a layman Nehemiah is concerned. Nehemiah as a congregational member, could have put all the blame on the people in the city and said that they should have done this or that, but he didn't. He decided that he wanted to be an answer to a problem by reacting to the condition of the people. Be aware of people that pretend to be concerned about your problems because they might not be concerned about you at all; actually they might start rejoicing when it looks like you're falling. Also, be careful when you live totally by other people's compliments because eventually, your will and emotions will start to die by their criticism. Since Nehemiah was born into captivity, maybe this is why he had such a heart of concern for others that had been captive. When you have been delivered out of captivity from something that once had you bound, but then you realize that it was only the grace and power of God that brought you out. Now, you see someone else going through what you have been through, but you refuse to help them, can you honestly say that you have a "love for God".

"Brothers, if anyone is caught in any sin, you who are spiritual [that is, you who are responsive to the guidance of the Spirit] are to restore such a person in a spirit of gentleness [not with a sense of superiority or self-righteousness], keeping a watchful eye on yourself, so that you are not tempted as well."

Galatians 6:1 AMP

No one has the authority to judge another individual because you don't know what they have been or are currently going through that is causing them or have caused them to act or react the way they are responding. So, you must be careful in judging other believers in Christ when you don't know all the circumstances.

"As for the one whose faith is weak, accept him [into your fellowship], but not for [the purpose of] quarreling over his opinions. One man's faith permits him to eat everything, while the weak believer eats only vegetables [to avoid eating ritually unclean meat or something previously considered unclean]. The one who eats [everything] is not to look down on the one who does not eat, and the one who does not eat must not criticize or pass judgment on the one who eats [everything], for God has accepted him. Who are you to judge the servant of another? Before his own master he stands [approved] or falls [out of favor]. And he [who serves the Master—

the "Lord] will stand, for the "Lord is able to make him stand."

Romans 14:1-4 AMP

"Make allowance for each other's faults and forgive anyone who offends you. Remember, the "Lord forgave you, so you must forgive others."

Colossians 3:13 NLT

Nehemiah did not want to make a move without praying first and to get a strategy from God! In chapter two Nehemiah had request permission from the king to return to Jerusalem, to look at the city, and to encourage the people to build the wall. Nehemiah was a man of honor; he had a political job as a cupbearer to the king. Nehemiah's job as a cupbearer was to taste anything brought to the king, such as if a glass of wine was brought to the king. Nehemiah tastes it first, and if nothing happens to him, then the king will drink the wine. So, as you can see the job of a cupbearer can be very dangerous. Since Nehemiah was the kings Cupbearer, he had to be in the presence of the king all the time. Nehemiah stayed in the land of his captivity, hoping that someday he might be able to use his position to help his people. Nehemiah is preparing to make a request of the king, but he is not ready. Since he had received the bad news about the Jews in the land, he has been fasting, mourning, and praying. The king noticed that Nehemiah was not himself. Nehemiah did not know that his feelings showed. He had tried to cover up the way he felt but was not able to. The king asks Nehemiah a question, why is your face sad since you are not sick? Nehemiah said, "May the king live forever" As a cupbearer he was able to say this with confidence, since he was the one that always tasted what came before the king. Nehemiah finally was able to tell the king what was bothering him. Nehemiah said to the king, "the city of my fathers is in trouble". Nehemiah continues, and gets right to the point when talking to the king and saying, "So I prayed to the God of heaven". The king knew that Nehemiah wanted to ask him something more, so then Nehemiah continued to speak, and asked the king to grant him a leave of absence to go to Jerusalem to help rebuild the city. Nehemiah was a young man who did not waste words, so when the king asked him when he was going to be back, he gave him a time. Nehemiah knew that he had a difficult trip ahead of him as he had to travel through dangerous countries, so he asks the king for letters of introduction and explanation to the governors along his route so they would give protection as he traveled through their lands. It was customary in many parts of the east to obtain letters of recommendation, or orders for safe conduct, when the traveler desired to visit different districts under one central authority. Without the letters he could not travel in comfort of safety; but having them to present to the different districts meant that they were bound to protect him. Even though Nehemiah trusted God, he still did not mind asking the king for his official assistance and protection along the route. The King had sent part of the

Persia army to accompany Nehemiah on his journey. When Nehemiah reached his destination, he was already starting to face opposition. Sanballat the Horonite, Tobiah the Ammonite, and Geshem the Arabian were three men who were the enemies of God and his people. They tried to stop the building of the temple, and now they are trying to stop the rebuilding of the wall. When Nehemiah showed up in the city with part of the Persia army, everybody in the country had heard about it and wanted to know who this man with all these people is. They were told that he was a cupbearer to the king of Persia, and that he was coming to help the Jews. When word went out throughout the country of what Nehemiah had come to do, the enemy was upset. When Nehemiah arrived in Jerusalem, he did not want to cause any problems, so he went out at nighttime by himself for the inspection of the land to see what the real condition was. There was so much debris on the ground that Nehemiah's horse did not even have a path to travel, so he had to get off his horse. Nehemiah always uses good judgment in doing God's work. After Nehemiah surveyed and did an evaluation of the work that needed to be done on the land. Nehemiah called a meeting of the leaders in the surrounding area of Jerusalem. He shared with them how God had led him to take a leave of absence and come to Jerusalem. He shared with the leaders that he had already made his inspection and knew the situation of the land. Nehemiah said with confidence "Let's do this job. God is with us." and they all replied, "Let us rise up and build". When Sanballat the Horonite, Tobiah the

Servant, the Ammonite, and Geshem the Arabian heard about what was getting ready to happen, they laughed. The enemy will always use different methods to discourage you.

Chapter three talks about one of the greatest building projects in Jerusalem, which was the rebuilding of the walls. Ezra and Zerubbabel were led back to the land to rebuild the temple. Which means that their assignment was different from the assignment that had been given to Nehemiah. Nehemiah's assignment as a layman was to rebuild the wall and gates of Jerusalem. Isn't it amazing how God gives different assignments to everyone to accomplish His purpose? Most people when they start something new, they always start out imitating someone else, and after going through trial and error most people find out the best thing to do, is to be yourself. There are 10 gates that represent the rebuilding of the walls of Jerusalem. These ten gates are planted in scripture to explain the "GOSPEL PLAN OF SALVATION".

- ♣ Sheep gate
- ♣ Fish gate
- ♣ Old gate
- ♣ Valley gate
- ♣ Dung gate
- ♣ Gates of the fountain
- ♣ Watergate

- ♣ Horse Gate
- ♣ East gate
- ♣ Gate Miphkad

SHEEP GATE

The sheep gate is where everything begins for Nehemiah, because this was his entrance into Jerusalem.

"After this there was a feast of the Jews, and Jesus went up to Jerusalem. Now there is in Jerusalem by the Sheep Gate a pool, which is called in Hebrew, Bethesda, having five porches. In these lay a great multitude of sick people, blind, lame, paralyzed, waiting for the moving of the water. For an angel went down at a certain time into the pool and stirred up the water; then whoever stepped in first, after the stirring of the water, was made well of whatever disease he had. Now a certain man was there who had an infirmity thirty-eight years. When Jesus saw him lying there, and knew that he already had been in that condition a long time, He said to him, "Do you want to be made well?" The sick man answered Him, "Sir, I have no man to put me into the pool when the water is stirred up; but while I am coming, another steps down before me." Jesus said to him, "Rise, take up your bed and walk." And immediately the man was made well, took up his bed, and walked. And that day was the Sabbath. The Jews therefore said to him, who was cured, "It is the Sabbath; it is not lawful for you to carry your bed." He answered them, "He who made me well said to me, 'Take up your bed and walk." Then they asked him, "Who is the Man who said to you, 'Take up your bed and walk'?" But the one who was healed did not know who it was; for Jesus had withdrawn, a multitude being in that place. Afterward, Jesus found him in the temple, and said to him, "See, you have been made well. Sin no more, lest a worse thing come upon you." The man departed and told the Jews that it was Jesus who had made him well."

John 5:1-15 NKJV

The sheep gate is also where the animals were brought through for sacrifice:

"The next day John saw Jesus coming toward him, and said, "Behold! The Lamb of God who takes away the sin of the world!"

John 1:29 NKJV

In person Jesus is the Lamb of God and his word is what takes away the sins of the world, so the sheep gate symbolizes: "THE CROSS OF CHRIST" The cross is the only place you can begin with God; it is your starting line of salvation and your finish line of sin. God does not ask you anything until you except his son Jesus Christ as your savior. God does not want your good works, your money or material possessions but instead he wants you, because he has something to give you which is eternal life and all of this begins at the sheep gate which is; "THE CROSS OF CHRIST" It reminds me of the lyrics of a song that goes as follows; "At the cross at the cross where I first realized and the burdens of my heart rolled away it was there by faith I receive my site and now I am happy all day"

FISH GATE

This is where the fish from the Jordan and the Sea of Galilee were brought through, into Jerusalem, located at the north wall. The Fish Gate was one place you would not have any problem locating people. Why, because this is the place where people hang out. So, the fish gate symbolizes; "PEOPLE"

"And Jesus, walking by the Sea of Galilee, saw two brothers, Simon called Peter, and Andrew his brother, casting a net into the sea; for they were fishermen. Then He said to them, "Follow Me, and I will make you fishers of men." They immediately left their nets and followed Him. Going on from there, he saw two other brothers, James, the son of Zebedee, and John, his brother, on the boat with Zebedee, their father, mending their nets. He called them, and immediately they left the boat and their father, and followed Him."

Matthew 4:18-22 NKJV

"Then He said to them, "These are the words which I spoke to you while I was still with you, that all things must be fulfilled which were written in the Law of Moses and the Prophets and the Psalms concerning Me." And He opened their understanding, that they might comprehend the Scriptures. Then He said to them, "Thus it is written, and thus it was necessary for the Christ to suffer and to rise from the dead the third day, and that repentance and remission of sins should be preached in His name to all nations, beginning at Jerusalem. And you are witnesses of these things. Behold, I send the Promise of My Father upon you; but tarry in the city of Jerusalem until you are endued with power from on high.""

Luke 24:44- 49 NKJV

He shared with every one of his disciples to be an effective witness; he told them to "Do not move until you are baptized, Indwelt, Regenerated and filled with the Holy Spirit" And according to scripture on the day of Pentecost, they were given power and authorize to become fishers of men.

"And being assembled together with them, He commanded them not to depart from Jerusalem, but to wait for the Promise of the Father, "which," He said, "you have heard from Me; for John truly baptized with water, but you shall be baptized with the Holy Spirit not many days from now." Therefore, when they had come together, they asked Him, saying, ""Lord, will You at this time restore the kingdom to Israel?" And He said to them, "It is not for you to know times or seasons which the Father has put in His own authority. But you shall receive power when the Holy Spirit has come upon you; and you shall be witnesses to Me in Jerusalem, and in all Judea and Samaria, and to the end of the earth.""

Acts 1:4-8 NKJV

The question that you might be wondering is, how did the disciples get this power? It was through prayer, I remember growing up in church and some of the elderly women in the church, were called mothers and the some of the elderly men were known as deacons and would say phrases like; Much prayer much power, little prayer little power". It was vitally important that before the disciples did anything, they had to have the power of the Holy Spirit working through and on them.

"Then they returned to Jerusalem from the mount called Olivet, which is near Jerusalem, a Sabbath day's journey. And when they entered, they went up into the upper room where they were staying Peter, James, John, and Andrew; Philip and Thomas; Bartholomew and Matthew; James the son of Alphaeus and Simon the Zealot; and Judas the son of James. These all continued with one accord in prayer and supplication, with the women and Mary the mother of Jesus, and with His brothers."

Acts 1:12-14 NKJV

"When the Day of Pentecost had fully come, they were all with one accord in one place. And suddenly there came a sound from heaven, as of a rushing mighty wind, and it filled the whole house where they were sitting. Then there appeared to them divided tongues, as of fire, and one sat upon each of them. And they were all filled with the Holy Spirit and began to speak with other tongues, as the Spirit gave them utterance."

Acts 2:1-4 NKJV

God is not requiring a non-believer to be a fisher of men because a non-believer would not know what God is talking about, but as a believer in Christ. "He wants you to go proclaim the Gospel to the non-believers. There are different ways to proclaim the Gospel, so there has to be different bait to catch different fish. Every fish will not bite off the same bait.

"Next to them the Tekoites made repairs; but their nobles did not put their shoulders to the work of their "Lord."

Nehemiah 3:5 NKJV

Now Nobles were individuals who thought that they were too good to do the work, or they always had an excuse and have refused to do the assignment that God told them to do, it's also very important to know that the nobles were right next to the fish gate, which means they were ready to be witness to.

"He that withholdeth corn, the people shall curse him: but blessing shall be upon the head of him that selleth it."

Proverbs 11:26 KJV

The word corn in the scripture represents the word of God, and anyone who holds back the word of God from someone that is hungry, is not being an effective witness; as a matter of fact, they are not being a witness for Christ at all.

OLD GATE

- ♣ A son of a goldsmith
- ♣ A son of a pharmacist
- ♣ Daughters of a father

"Moreover, Jehoiada the son of Paseah and Meshullam the son of Besodeiah repaired the Old Gate; they laid its beams and hung its doors, with its bolts and bars. And next to them Melatiah the Gibeonite, Jadon the Meronothite, the men of Gibeon and Mizpah, repaired the residence of the governor of the region beyond the river."

Nehemiah 3:6-7 NKJV

"Thus says the "LORD: "Stand in the ways and see, and ask for the old paths, where the good way is, and walk in it; Then you will find rest for your souls. But they said, 'We will not walk in it.'"

Jeremiah 6:16 NKJV

"Come to Me, all you who labor and are heavy laden, and I will give you rest. Take My yoke upon you and learn from Me, for I am gentle and lowly in heart, and you will find rest for your souls. For My yoke is easy and My burden is light.""

Matthew 11:28-30 NKJV

The third gate that is mentioned is known as the "old gate" which symbolizes: "REST IN CHRIST"

"Next to him Uzziel the son of Harhaiah, one of the goldsmiths, made repairs. Also next to him Hananiah, one of the perfumers, made repairs; and they fortified Jerusalem as far as the Broad Wall."

Nehemiah 3:8 NKJV

The weight of the stones in the walls of Jerusalem were extremely heavy and the son of a goldsmith is only used to sitting down and working with small pieces of gold not large stones. So even though the work was hard in building the walls of Jerusalem they did not quit, when most people are given a hard assignment especially when it is out of their comfort zone will slow down on the assignment that they have been given and eventually quit working, but the Word of God sent to empower you.

"And let us not grow weary while doing good, for in due season we shall reap if we do not lose heart."

Galatians 6:9 NKJV

Whenever God gives you an assignment to do that will enhance your community, city, state and the world, he doesn't want you to rely on your own strength, but he wants you to meditate and speak his word to yourself that says,

"I can do all things through Christ who strengthens me."

Philippians 4:13 NKJV

"No weapon formed against you shall prosper, and every tongue which rises against you in judgment You shall condemn. This is the heritage of the servants of the "LORD, and their righteousness is from Me," Says the "LORD."

Isaiah 54:17 NKJV

It is God's ability on your availability to accomplish the assignment that you have been giving. You might not ever be in the newspaper, on television or the radio but always remember one thing, that God is taking note of everything that he has ask you to do and what you're trying to figure out, God has already worked it out all you have to do is walk it out.

"And next to him was Shallum the son of Hallohesh, leader of half the district of Jerusalem; he and his daughters made repairs."

Nehemiah 3:12 NKJV

Shallum did not have any sons, so his daughters went to work helping him build the walls of Jerusalem. It was not only men that built the walls of Jerusalem but as you can see women also were involved. Some people will try to stop a woman from doing certain works of the "Lord, but God said that the woman is just as important as the men, especially in situations where there are not any men to do the work.

VALLEY GATE

Where the "sheep gate" is the "entrance into Jerusalem" the "valley gate" is the "exit out of Jerusalem" which leads down into the valley. Once you come to Christ through the "sheep gate" you must live your life through the "valley gate" most of your greatest growth since you have been a born-again believer in Christ have come through walking in the valleys of life.

"The “Lord is my shepherd; I shall not want. He makes me to lie down in green pastures; He leads me beside the still waters. He restores my soul; He leads me in the paths of righteousness For His name’s sake. Yea, though I walk through the valley of the shadow of death, I will fear no evil; For You are with me; Your rod and Your staff, they comfort me.”

Psalms 23:1-4 NKJV

God will lead you through your trials and difficulties in life so that he can empower, equip and elevate you to your next level in him, then you will be able to graduate from one stage of life to another. Faith must be developed to be strong. Humility needs to come from the inside because it is the fruit of the Holy Spirit. A lot of times when you are given an assignment to do for God, it is vitally important to make sure that you keep a humble heart. Most people work their assignment with an arrogant type of mentality but after going through stages throughout life of the assignment not working out, they eventually realize that the assignment that they had been giving, had nothing to do with their expertise in the first place. When God gives you an assignment to do it's not just for you but ultimately it is for the people you will come in contact with. We must continue to share the gospel through words and or actions but remember that God works through an individual who has a humble heart. So, the "valley gate" symbolizes "THE GATE OF HUMBLENESS".

"And whoever exalts himself will be humbled, and he who humbles himself will be exalted."

Matthew 23:12 NKJV

DUNG GATE

"Malchijah the son of Rechab, leader of the district of Beth Haccerem, repaired the Refuse Gate; he built it and hung its doors with its bolts and bars."

Nehemiah 3:14 NKJV

This is a very important gate for the health of the city but not much to say about this gate. This is the gate were the "GARBAGE WAS PASS THROUGH".

"Therefore, having these promises, beloved, let us cleanse ourselves from all filthiness of the flesh and spirit, perfecting holiness in the fear of God."

II Corinthians 7:1 NKJV

How can you as a born-again believer throw out fleshly and spiritual garbage out of your life so that you can live a life pleasing to God?

"If we confess our sins, He is faithful and just to forgive us our sins and to cleanse us from all unrighteousness."

I John 1:9 NKJV

FOUNTAIN GATE

"Shallun the son of Col-Hozeh, leader of the district of Mizpah, repaired the Fountain Gate; he built it, covered it, hung its doors with its bolts and bars, and repaired the wall of the Pool of Shelah by the King's Garden, as far as the stairs that go down from the City of David."

Nehemiah 3:15 NKJV

The fountain gate refers to the "WOMAN AT THE WELL"

"But whoever drinks of the water that I shall give him will never thirst. But the water that I shall give him will become in him a fountain of water springing up into everlasting life.""

John 4:14 NKJV

"He who believes in Me, as the Scripture has said, out of his heart will flow rivers of living water.""

John 7:38 NKJV

In the next verse John explains his statement:

"But this He spoke concerning the Spirit, whom those believing in Him would receive; for the Holy Spirit was not yet given, because Jesus was not yet glorified."

John 7:39 NKJV

In Romans chapter eight verse nine it says:

"But you are not in the flesh but in the Spirit, if indeed the Spirit of God dwells in you. Now if anyone does not have the Spirit of Christ, he is not His."

Romans 8:9 NKJV

As a born-again believer in Christ once you are filled with the spirit of God you are not just a well, but you have now become a fountain of living water to be a blessing to every- one that you come in contact with.

WATER GATE

"Moreover, the Nethinim who dwelt in Ophel made repairs as far as the place in front of the Water Gate toward the east, and on the projecting tower."

Nehemiah 3:26 NKJV

The water gate was the gate used to bring "water into the city". Even though the aqueduct brought water into the city, it did not bring all of it. An aqueduct is defined as; "A conduit or artificial channel for conducting water from a distance, usually by means of gravity. A bridge like structure that carries a water conduit or canal across a valley or over a river" so the remainder of the water was carried through the water gate. The water gate symbolizes the "WORD OF GOD". Ezra read the word of God from the water gate which I believe was the plan of God.

"You are already clean because of the word which I have spoken to you."

John 15:3 NKJV

"Sanctify them by Your truth. Your word is truth."

John 17:17 NKJV

It's through the water gate how we spread the Word of God. When I played football, we always use to have the managers of the sport team to make sure all the players stayed refresh with plenty of water. Why? Because the players were thirsty, and it was the job of the person that was in charge of the water to make sure that everyone that was thirsty received some water to cure their thirst. As the manager is to a sport team so it is with you as a disciple of Christ. As born-again believers in Jesus Christ we are the individuals that are carrying the water, which is the word of God and are thirsty for God's word, you are the supplier to take care of their thirst by suppling the word of God, which the end result is eternal life. An important note to know about the water gate is that it was not repaired. The reason why the water gate was not repaired was because, when the other gates and walls were torn down, the water gate remained intact. It did not need any repairs at all which means that when it comes to the word of God it never needs any repairs it is always intact. What God wants you to do is not get caught in conversations defending the gospel because the gospel will always defend itself. Your assignment is to spread the gospel through-out the nations and as you are going allow the gospel to make disciples.

HORSE GATE

A horse was an animal that was rode by a warrior. Horses are also symbolic of powers making wars. Jesus' rode into Jerusalem on a donkey, which did not make him seem like he was not a warrior because he was on a donkey. A donkey was the animal that was rode by kings, so it was not considered a humble little animal in that day. The horse gate is symbolic of a "SOLDIERS SERVICE" of believers in Jesus Christ.

"I saw by night, and behold, a man riding on a red horse, and it stood among the myrtle trees in the hollow; and behind him were horses: red, sorrel, and white."

Zechariah 1:8 NKJV

"Another horse, fiery red, went out. And it was granted to the one who sat on it to take peace from the earth, and that people should kill one another; and there was given to him a great sword."

Revelation 6:4 NKJV

"I, therefore, the prisoner of the "Lord, beseech you to walk worthy of the calling with which you were called,"

Ephesians 4:1 NKJV

"Finally, my brethren, be strong in the "Lord and in the power of His might. Put on the whole armor of God, that you may be able to stand against the wiles of the devil. For we do not wrestle against flesh and blood, but against principalities, against powers, against the rulers of the darkness of this age, against spiritual hosts of wickedness in the heavenly places. Therefore, take up the whole armor of God, that you may be able to withstand in the evil day, and having done all, to stand. Stand therefore, having girded your waist with truth, having put on the breastplate of righteousness, and having shod your feet with the preparation of the gospel of peace; above all, taking the shield of faith with which, you will be able to quench all the fiery darts of the wicked one. And take the helmet of salvation, and the sword of the Spirit, which is the word of God;"

Ephesians 6:10-17 NKJV

"You therefore must endure hardship as a good soldier of Jesus Christ."

II Timothy 2:3 NKJV

As a believer in Christ there are going to be battles you must fight but the good news is that you have been equipped to fight.

EAST GATE

The east gate is a gate of "ANTICIPATION AND EXCITEMENT". This gate as you would expect is located on the east side of the city and was the first one that was open in the morning. The east gate in Jerusalem is sealed and it is facing in the direction of were the sun rises. During the night the watchman was on the wall, walking up and down, making his rounds. Early in the morning the watchman comes around to the east gate and watches for the sun to arise for a sign of the beginning of the day. At night the people that were trying to sleep would often wonder if the enemy is out at night. They would often ask the watchmen at night, when is nighttime going to end? The watchman would always respond by saying, "It's still dark but morning is coming" but as soon as the light comes, he then will give a signal and shouts out, "There's light out here and I can see that there is no enemy". As believers we should all be at the east gate.

"For the "Lord Himself will descend from heaven with a shout, with the voice of an archangel, and with the trumpet of God. And the dead in Christ will rise first. Then we who are alive and remain shall be caught up together with them in the clouds to meet the "Lord in the air. And thus, we shall always be with the "Lord."

I Thessalonians 4:16-17 NKJV

This scripture is referring to the rapture because Jesus is going to come take his own out of the world before the sun comes up. Notice in verse thirty that Meshullam repaired the part over against the chamber where he lived. You might not be able to travel the world, you might not be able to reach your neighborhood; but you can reach and give the word of God to your family! It is ultimately your responsibility to get the gospel out to your family. Your assignment as a believer is not to get people saved, Jesus will take care of that.

6 I planted, Apollos watered, but God gave the increase.

1 Corinthians 3:6 NKJV

You are called to just deliver the gospel so that people can hear it! "How then shall they call on Him in whom they have not believed? And how shall they believe in Him of whom they have not heard? And how shall they hear without a preacher? And how shall they preach unless they are sent? As it is written: "How beautiful are the feet of those who preach the gospel of peace, who bring glad tidings of good things!" But they have not all obeyed the gospel. For Isaiah says, ""LORD, who has believed our report?" So, then faith comes by hearing, and hearing by the word of God."

Romans 10:14-17 NKJV

GATE MIPHKAD

Means "REVIEW" or "REGISTRY". When a stranger came to Jerusalem, he had to have a visa, not like those we have today, but he had to stop at this gate and register. It was also a gate of review, When the army had been out fighting a battle and returned, they passed through this gate. This is the gate that David reviewed his soldiers returning from battle. When they passed through this arch, David was there to thank his men for their unselfish loyalty.

In First Thessalonians it says, "For the "Lord Himself will descend from heaven with a shout, with the voice of an archangel, and with the trumpet of God. And the dead in Christ will rise first. Then we who are alive and remain shall be caught up together with them in the clouds to meet the "Lord in the air. And thus, we shall always be with the "Lord."

I Thessalonians 4:16-17 NKJV

During the rapture individuals that were believers in Christ and have experience physically death will rise up first and the believers that are remaining will be caught up to meet the "Lord in the air. After the rapture as believers in Christ we are all going to appear before the judgement seat of Christ. I want to bring to your attention that this Judgement is not the same as the Great White Throne that is mentioned in the book of revelation where it says.

"Then I saw a great white throne and Him who sat on it, from whose face the earth and the heaven fled away. And there was found no place for them. And I saw the dead, small and great, standing before God, and books were opened. And another book was opened, which is the Book of Life. And the dead were judged according to their works, by the things which were written in the books. The sea gave up the dead who were in it, and Death and Hades delivered up the dead who were in them. And they were judged, each one according to his works. Then Death and Hades were cast into the lake of fire. This is the second death. And anyone not found written in the Book of Life was cast into the lake of fire."

Revelation 20:11-15 NKJV

To make sure that these three separate judgements are not combine into one general judgement, three different thrones are mentioned. There can be no "General Judgement" because the Scriptures speak of one judgment as being in the "Air".

FIRST JUDGEMENT THE "JUDGEMENT SEAT OF CHRIST" IN THE AIR FOR "BELIEVERS ONLY"

So, we are always confident, knowing that while we are at home in the body, we are absent from the "Lord. For we walk by faith, not by sight. We are confident, yes, well pleased rather to be absent from the body and to be present with the "Lord. Therefore, we make it our aim, whether present or absent, to be well pleasing to Him. For we must all appear before the judgment seat of Christ, that each one may receive the things done in the body, according to what he has done, whether good or bad."

II Corinthians 5:6-10 NKJV

"But why do you judge your brother? Or why do you show contempt for your brother? For we shall all stand before the judgment seat of Christ."

Romans 14:10 NKJV

This judgement is for believers as pertains to "sin"

"There is therefore now no condemnation to those who are in Christ Jesus, who do not walk according to the flesh, but according to the Spirit. For the law of the Spirit of life in Christ Jesus has made me free from the law of sin and death. For what the law could not do in that it was weak through the flesh, God did by sending His own Son in the likeness of sinful flesh, on account of sin: He condemned sin in the flesh, that the righteous requirement of the law might be fulfilled in us who do not walk according to the flesh but according to the Spirit."

Romans 8:1-4 NKJV

""Most assuredly, I say to you, he who hears My word and believes in Him who sent Me has everlasting life, and shall not come into judgment, but has passed from death into life."

John 5:24 NKJV

As a born-again believer this judgement as a sinner is past and was settled at the cross. As soon as an unbeliever accepts Jesus into their life the sin question has been settle. The following verses will explain the transition from a "sinner" to a "son".

"But He was wounded for our transgressions, He was bruised for our iniquities; The chastisement for our peace was upon Him, And by His stripes we are healed. All we like sheep have gone astray; We have turned, everyone, to his own way; And the "LORD has laid on Him the iniquity of us all."

Isaiah 53:5-6 NKJV

If your iniquities are on Jesus, then that means the iniquities are not on you. "Sin" and "Sins" are both different. Jesus Christ death on the cross was for your sin. Sin is the tendency within a person to do wrong.

Your sin tendency now has a counteracting force called the "New Nature".

"Therefore, if anyone is in Christ, he is a new creation; old things have passed away; behold, all things have become new."

II Corinthians 5:17 NKJV

You now have a dual personality of the "Old Nature" and "New Nature" and the nature that you feed will always dominate the nature that is starved. There will always be a warfare between the two natures until the old nature is eradicated at death.

"Watch and pray, lest you enter into temptation. The spirit indeed is willing, but the flesh is weak.""

Matthew 26:41 NKJV

"Now the works of the flesh are evident, which are: adultery, fornication, uncleanness, lewdness, idolatry, sorcery, hatred, contentions, jealousies, outbursts of wrath, selfish ambitions, dissensions, heresies, envy, murders, drunkenness, revelries, and the like; of which I tell you beforehand, just as I also told you in time past, that those who practice such things will not inherit the kingdom of God."

Galatians 5:19-21 NKJV

"Sins" are the outward acts of doing wrong, that are committed as a result of your "sin" nature and have to be put away daily by confession.

"If we confess our sins, He is faithful and just to forgive us our sins and to cleanse us from all unrighteousness."

I John 1:9 NKJV

The judgement as "sons" is for "unconfessed sins"

"My little children, these things I write to you, so that you may not sin. And if anyone sins, we have an Advocate with the Father, Jesus Christ the righteous."

I John 2:1 NKJV

"And you have forgotten the exhortation which speaks to you as to sons: "My son, do not despise the chastening of the "LORD, nor be discouraged when you are rebuked by Him; For whom the "LORD loves He chastens, and scourges every son whom He receives." If you endure chastening, God deals with you as with sons; for what son is there whom a father does not chasten? But if you are without chastening, of which all have become partakers, then you are illegitimate and not sons. Furthermore, we have had human fathers who corrected us, and we paid them respect. Shall we not much more readily be in subjection to the Father of spirits and live? For they indeed for a few days chastened us as seemed best to them, but He for our profit, that we may be partakers of His holiness. Now no chastening seems to be joyful for the present, but painful; nevertheless, afterward it yields the peaceable fruit of righteousness to those who have been trained by it."

Hebrews 12:5-11 NKJV

SECOND JUDGEMENT

THE "THRONE OF GLORY" ON THE EARTH FOR THE NATIONS "

"When the Son of Man comes in His glory, and all the holy angels with Him, then He will sit on the throne of His glory. All the nations will be gathered before Him, and He will separate them one from another, as a shepherd divides his sheep from the goats. And He will set the sheep on His right hand, but the goats on the left. Then the King will say to those on His right hand, 'Come, you blessed of My Father, inherit the kingdom prepared for you from the foundation of the world: for I was hungry and you gave Me food; I was thirsty and you gave Me drink; I was a stranger and you took Me in; I was naked and you clothed Me; I was sick and you visited Me; I was in prison and you came to Me.' "Then the righteous will answer Him, saying, '"Lord, when did we see You hungry and feed You, or thirsty and give You drink? When did we see You a stranger and take You in, or naked and clothe You? Or when did we see You sick, or in prison, and come to You?' And the King will answer and say to them, 'Assuredly, I say to you, inasmuch as you did it to one of the least of these My brethren, you did it to Me.' "Then He will also say to those on the left hand, 'Depart from Me, you cursed, into the everlasting fire prepared for the devil and his angels: for I was hungry and you gave Me no food; I was thirsty and you gave Me no drink; I was a stranger and you did not take Me in, naked and you did not clothe Me, sick and in prison and you did not visit Me.' "Then they also will answer Him, saying, "'Lord, when did we see You hungry or thirsty or a stranger or naked or sick or in prison, and did not minister to You?' Then He will answer them, saying, 'Assuredly, I say to you, inasmuch as you did not do it to one of the least of these, you did not do it to Me.' And these will go away into everlasting punishment, but the righteous into eternal life.""

Matthew 25:31- 46 NKJV

THE THIRD JUDGMENT THE "GREAT WHITE THRONE" IN HEAVEN THE DEAD

"Then I saw a great white throne and Him who sat on it, from whose face the earth and the heaven fled away. And there was found no place for them. And I saw the dead, small and great, standing before God, and books were opened. And another book was opened, which is the Book of Life. And the dead were judged according to their works, by the things which were written in the books. The sea gave up the dead who were in it, and Death and Hades delivered up the dead who were in them. And they were judged, each one according to his works. Then Death and Hades were cast into the lake of fire. This is the second death. And anyone not found written in the Book of Life was cast into the lake of fire."

Revelation 20:11-15 NKJV

Remember that only believers in Christ will be present at the judgement seat of Christ because this judgement is not about receiving salvation but rewards for things you've done on earth. Paul took these rewards very serious by what he had stated in the following verse.

"Knowing, therefore, the terror of the "Lord, we persuade men; but we are well known to God, and I also trust are well known in your consciences."

II Corinthians 5:11 NKJV

Paul knew that he needed to stay busy because eventually he was going to have to turn in a report about his work. Paul wanted a good report reflecting his work. Paul wanted a report of serving and reaching out to others sixty minutes in every hour, twenty-four hours a day or seven days a week. This is what miphkad is, God is taken a review on what you did on earth. Did you evangelize to every person possible; did you go out "make disciples"? David knew his men that was scarred from battle and what they had done. David would call out his men and say, I have a reward for you. As David called out his men to give rewards to them, there will also be many believers called out before the judgement seat of Christ to receive their rewards. One important thing that I want you to realize is that the rewards giving at the judgement seat of Christ is not just given to the five ministerial gifts to the church, which are.

"And He Himself gave some to be apostles, some prophets, some evangelists, and some pastors and teachers,"

Ephesians 4:11 NKJV

Remember, that Nehemiah had no ministerial title he was a lay person or congregation member who had a heart of passion to reach out within his city to make a difference. Nehemiah also knew that along with making an "Impact there will always be an attack" but that didn't stop him he just kept moving forward with the plan. You don't need a title in front of your name or letters behind your name to evangelize all you need to do is be obedient and do what God has given you to do, which is to "Go make disciples by witnessing to them with the gospel of Jesus Christ" At the writing of this book I have been sharing the gospel for over twenty-nine years and have always empowered believers by telling them that the day you became born-again you received your Bachelors (B.A.),When you were touched by Jesus, the Master teacher you have received your Masters (M.A.) and when you were empowered by the Power of the Holy Spirit and been Delivered, you have received your (P.H.D.).

"But you shall receive power when the Holy Spirit has come upon you; and you shall be witnesses to Me in Jerusalem, and in all Judea and Samaria, and to the end of the earth.""

Acts 1:8 NKJV

Peter and John did not have a physical degree but they each had a spiritual degree, which is the degree that really matters that comes from spending time with Jesus.

"Now when they saw the boldness of Peter and John, and perceived that they were uneducated and untrained men, they marveled. And they realized that they had been with Jesus."

Acts 4:13 NKJV

"And between the upper room at the corner, as far as the Sheep Gate, the goldsmiths and the merchants made repairs."

Nehemiah 3:32 NKJV

We have been through ten gates and it's amazing that we are right back to gate number one, we have also been all the way around the walls of Jerusalem, and we are right back where we started "The Sheep Gate". Remember, that the "sheep gate" symbolizes the "Cross of Christ".

In Chapter 3 Nehemiah uses a strategy to get the wall around Jerusalem built. Different people were place in a certain section of the wall to repair, so that the wall was going up all the way around the city at the same time. In this chapter we will see that the wall was built halfway up. The enemy found that the weapon of laughter did not stop the work, so now they are going to try a new method to try to stop the building of the wall. The laughter did not stop them from building as a matter of fact the building progress more so now the enemy will use the weapon of ridicule in front of others. The children of Israel were starting to question themselves; they began to start wondering if they would be able to complete the wall. Tobiah the Ammonite started began to give them discouraging remarks,

"Now Tobiah the Ammonite was beside him, and he said, "Whatever they build, if even a fox goes up on it, he will break down their stone wall.""

Nehemiah 4:3 NKJV

A Fox can walk over ground and not leave much of a track, a fox can also run on a wall and not disturb a thing on it. Tobiah knew that the builders were goldsmiths, druggist, and women. What do you think Nehemiah is going to do? You got it, he prayed. The men who tried to hinder the building, were God's enemies as well as the Jews enemies. Under the law, the Jews had a perfect right to ask for justice. They were correct to ask that a righteous judgement be made. However, Jesus Christ has reversed the right to ask for justice for all believers. We are told to forgive, read the following scriptures.

“And be kind to one another, tenderhearted, forgiving one another, even as God in Christ forgave you.”

Ephesians 4:32 NKJV

“Beloved, do not avenge yourselves, but rather give place to wrath; for it is written, “Vengeance is Mine, I will repay,” says the “Lord.”

Romans 12:19 NKJV

As a believer in Christ and according to the word of God we are supposed to walk in faith. Nehemiah ignored the attacks by the enemy, prayed to God and continue to build. When the enemy saw that laughing at them did not stop the building of the wall, they became very angry and begin to move in another direction but once again we see that prayer was Nehemiah source. At first Nehemiah prayed but this time they were "Watching and praying". Nehemiah knew that trusting in the “Lord did not mean to sit around and be stagnate and do nothing. He knew that when you trust the “Lord you are doing something while you are trusting. Nehemiah knew that the enemy was plotting to come against him, so he set a watch. Not only was there trouble on the outside but on the inside as well. The devil can hurt you severely from the inside. One of Devils greatest weapons against believers is discouragement. The enemy took advantage of the Jews discouragement, and they planned a surprise attack. "We are going to take them when they are not looking for us". Nehemiah had a strategic plan against a surprise attack. He decided to put every man in position where he could defend his own family, which made him more comfortable when he was re-building the walls of Jerusalem. With his family at home, some distance away from him, a builder did not know whether or not they were safe. So, Nehemiah put them with their families and armed them well". The enemy eventually retired once they found out that they could not surprise an attack on the Jews.

While Nehemiah was in the process of rebuilding the walls of Jerusalem, he encounters opposition. First the enemy laughed at the Jews, then the enemy ridiculed them and finally there was open opposition. It was so tense that Nehemiah had his builders put trowel in one hand and a sword in the other hand while the worked on the wall. Nehemiah and all the men with him worked very hard. There was opposition coming from within and of course this is where devil always try to divide the people of God, if he can't work outside in then he will attempt to work inside out. The devil had already caused discouragement among the Jews, and now he is taking it a step farther and causes conflict within. Because the Jews were so busy building the walls, they did not have the opportunity to carry on their personal business they had to buy corn, food for their families, and in doing so they had to mortgage their property. Some of them had to mortgage their property to pay their taxes, taxes were high in that day. They were borrowing money from their own people. Nehemiah did not realize it, but the people wanted to build the walls of Jerusalem, so they very quietly mortgage their property. The enemy outside the walls was not able to harm them because there was so much love and harmony within but now there's conflict.

"Only let your conduct be worthy of the gospel of Christ, so that whether I come and see you or am absent, I may hear of your affairs, that you stand fast in one spirit, with one mind striving together for the faith of the gospel, and not in any way terrified by your adversaries, which is to them a proof of perdition, but to you of salvation, and that from God."

Philippians 1:27-28 NKJV

"For where envy and self-seeking exist, confusion and every evil thing are there."

James 3:16 NKJV

Up to this point Nehemiah had maintain his actions but now he becomes angry, and he was not just a little angry but very angry. Nehemiah openly rebuked the nobles and the rulers for their actions. Nehemiah expose those who had done wrong in the presence of the group. Nehemiah exposed the underhanded dealings with the people and was not quiet about the sin he uncovered, he definitely spoke out. Nehemiah expose the sin of his people in the open, and nobody was able to answer him they remained quiet while he was there. They are going to cause Nehemiah a lot of trouble when he goes back to the palace in Shushan, but Nehemiah continue to rebuild the walls of Jerusalem and serve God. Nehemiah knew that he was in a position where he could had benefited financially, which was a real test of his integrity, but he refuses to use his position for financial gain. His appeal to the wealthy Jews was to restore what they had collected and not to collect any more payments. When they said that they were going to do the restoration he did not believe them "so he had the take an oath, that they would do what they had promise." Although they were God's people, he knew better than to take them at their word's, so he required them to put the oath in writing. Remember now, Nehemiah is a government official and wore a uniform. He shook off his long rob in front of the crowd and said, "This is the way God will shake you out if you do not make your promise good". Paul said to the Galatians,

"I could wish that those who trouble you would even cut themselves off!"

Galatians 5:12 NKJV

He wanted the legalizers to be absolutely cut off because of the damage they were doing to the Galatian believers. Nehemiah had a right to receive a salary. Even though the governors before Nehemiah receive salaries, Nehemiah chose not to receive no financial gain at all. He regularly entertains one hundred and fifty guests. He also entertained Jews from surrounding nations who had come to live in the city but had not yet found a place to live. Apparently, he did all of this at his own expense. He was different from the other governors. He did not demand the governor's food allowance, because he had a heart for the others who were working hard around him.

Nehemiah concern was for his people, but they would forget him. Nehemiah asked God to remember him. It is so good to know that, while God does not remember our sins, He will always remember our good works.

Nehemiah encounter a lot of opposition while he was rebuilding the walls of Jerusalem. The devil is doing everything he can to cause Nehemiah to stumble, fall and stop so he would fail from rebuilding the wall. The devil is trying to do the same thing to a lot of "Believers in Christ" today, which is to make them stumble, fall and stop evangelizing in their communities, city, state and the world. It's sad to say there have been some believers who have allowed the enemy to distract and detour them from sharing the gospel to unbelievers. As you study the sixth chapter, you'll see that Nehemiah did not stop he kept rebuilding the wall. You will also notice that the wall is almost finish except for the doors. Sanballat, Tobiah, Geshem, and others heard that the wall was completed but Nehemiah admitted, that what was reported to them was not completely true because the gates were not set up. Since the enemy could not stop the work that Nehemiah was doing, they decided to work out a compromise with him, but their intention was not for the good of Nehemiah. The location where they wanted to have a meeting with Nehemiah was at Ono, but he turned down their invitation because he knew that they meant to harm him not help. Nehemiah knew that it would not be profitable for him to engage in a conversation with the enemy. Nehemiah sent messengers to them saying "I am doing a great work, so I cannot come down "The enemy wanted to compromise but Nehemiah said, "No". Nehemiah was doing a good work and did not have time to come down and waste his time with the enemy. Nehemiah made it very clear to the enemy that he had an uncompromising attitude. They continue to send for Nehemiah four more times and even Sanballat came a fifth time with a letter in his hand. The enemy was very persistent in trying to compromise with him. Nehemiah's presence in Jerusalem was very important for the completing of the wall but of course the enemy didn't care about that. Even though the letter had great wording and was very polite it was a "hook with bait on it". Why, because the letter contained a threat by accusing Nehemiah of attempting to rebel against Persia and set up a separate state was either been posted or through a verbal public announcement. This communication was designed to discourage the people that were working on the wall with him and accused him of wanting to become king. They accused him of not just wanting to become king but also said that he had hired prophets to support what he said. The enemy has now taken another step by trying to put pressure on Nehemiah to meet with them. Nehemiah's reaction to them regarding their accusations was, "You actually did not hear the things you are accusing me of; you made them up yourself". Nehemiah took his problem to God and said, "The enemy is doing all of this to try to hinder and stop me from doing your work but with your help, you will give me the strength to continue". Shemaiah who was a false prophet, pretends to have Nehemiah's best interest and safety at heart. He told Nehemiah that he wanted to reveal a plot against the governor's life and the temple was the only place that he would be safe. Even though Shemaiah was sharing all of this with him, what he did not realize is that Nehemiah had great spiritual insight. Nehemiah knew that God did not send him and that Tobiah and Sanballat had hired him. Nehemiah was consistently getting plotted by the enemy for his destruction. He continued to deal with people who pretended to be his friends, but he was still in a difficult spot. He is now in another plot scheme from the enemy, but he turns to God! Once again, the land was cursed by false prophets. Finally, the wall was finish in fifty-two days but even though the wall is finish there is still danger. The enemy is still persistent in his opposition by circulating letters to the nobles of Judah. Tobiah, who was a son-in-law, had married a daughter of one of the nobles whose name was Shechaniah. He had a straight line of connection from the outside to the inside the walls of Jerusalem and everything that Nehemiah did or said was reported to Tobiah. After receiving information, Tobiah would send letters to try and put fear in Nehemiah".

As we begin our reading in chapter seven, we will see that the wall has been completed. Now the people are beginning to protect the walls of Jerusalem. Many of the homes have already been built, but inside the city there is still a lot of work to be accomplish. As they are clearing out the debris, they also had to protect the city, because the enemy that tried to hinder the rebuilding of the walls would now like to destroy the city. After the walls were finish, Nehemiah set the doors at the different gates, and then he appointed porters, singers and Levites to protect the city. The porters were the watchmen, they were the ones who took care of the wall. They were on guard duty all around the wall, alerting the people who were on the inside of the wall, what was going on the outside of the wall. If the enemy or some other danger approached, they would sound the alarm. The porters' assignment was to watch day and night which means that it was a twenty-four-hour job. Even though the standards for the job of the porter were high, we'll find out that some of the rules that were set up were not enforced as they should have been. The guards at the wall were not supposed to show any partiality to who came and went inside the city walls. Having porters and singers made for a great city, but that is not all. Levites were also appointed, they were ministers. The scripture mentions a man name Hanani who was not Nehemiah's natural brother. Remember at the beginning of the book of Nehemiah, that while he was serving in the court of Artaxerxes one of his brothers from Jerusalem came and told him about the condition of the Remnant that had returned. He was one of Nehemiah's fellow Israelites not his natural brother. Hanani apparently was one of the leaders in Jerusalem, and it was him that informed Nehemiah about the conditions in Jerusalem. Nehemiah already knew Hanani therefore Nehemiah said in verse two "I gave my brother Hanani and Hananiah the ruler of the palace, charge over

Jerusalem. Because he knew him at the beginning in chapter one verse two. Hanani was one of the men placed in charge over Jerusalem because he "was a faithful man and feared God". Hanani might not had been educated but he was faithful. There is absolutely nothing wrong with been educated or having a higher education. I personally have a one masters' degree (Marriage and biblical family counseling) and two doctorates one in ministry (D.Min) and the other in theology (Th.D.) and my education have help me tremendously over the years but ultimately it was my faithfulness that has allowed me to teach people how to engage, be equip and empower for evangelism and outreach through-out the United States. The scripture states that Peter and John did amazing things not because of their education but because they spent quality time with Jesus.

"Now when they saw the boldness of Peter and John, and perceived that they were uneducated and untrained men, they marveled. And they realized that they had been with Jesus. And seeing the man who had been healed standing with them, they could say nothing against it."

Acts 4:13-14 NKJV

What God wants is your faithfulness. "Moreover, it is required in stewards that one be found faithful."

I Corinthians 4:2 NKJV

Can your Pastor depend on you? Can other born-again believers depend on you? Can your Husband or Wife depend on you? Can your children or other family members depend on you? What about your supervisor and co-workers, can they depend on you at your job? "Education is only profitable if you are faithful but if you are not faithful your education is stagnant" Each entrance into the city was to be watched during the day. At night, when anything could happen, everyone was to watch at least his own household. What this is showing us, is that God will hold you responsible for your own house. Not all of the building was completed at this time. It was possible that a man might become interested in building his own house and forget to watch. In the last verse of this chapter, we see that the children of Israel are back in the land, under the leadership of Nehemiah and a tremendous amount of work had been done. Nehemiah's work is not finish, there is still more to do.

In the previous chapter we saw that, after Nehemiah had prepared to go to guard the city, he appointed singers. He wanted to make sure that Jerusalem is continually filled with Joy. Not only was there joy in the city but he also wanted to make sure that they received the word of God, so all the people gather at the water gate to hear the word of God spoken by Ezra. The people that stood before Ezra was able to "hear the word of God with understanding" and were very focus on what was being said. The Israelites, who were in attendance, were extremely interested in the word, maybe because they have been in captivity for seventy years and had never heard the word of God. When Ezra read the word of God there was no one sitting, they remained standing as the word of God was read. As Ezra finish the speaking the word of God all the people lifted their hands and worship God then went down to the ground and touch their forehead to the ground. All the people were gathered by the water gate inside the walls of Jerusalem. There were men who placed in designated areas throughout the crowd, so when Ezra read a certain portion of the law, he would then stop to let each of the men who were at their designated spot throughout the congregation would ask his group, "Did you understand what was read". I would imagine some of them did understand and the others who did not understand what was spoken probably raised their hand to ask a question. Once the question was asked the person who was assigned to that group would explain what was spoken to them. Once every group understood the word then Ezra would continual to read the next portion of the law. The reading of the law, and the asking and answering of the questions from the people caused the people to understand the law. Many of the people had never heard the word of God. The word actually cause them to repent and be convicted of their sin. After hearing the word there was also joy through- out the city. When the word of God is preached it should always empower you to go do something nice for someone else verse ten says,"

"Then he said to them, "Go your way, eat the fat, drink the sweet, and send portions to those for whom nothing is prepared; for this day is holy to our "Lord. Do not sorrow, for the joy of the "LORD is your strength.""

Nehemiah 8:10 NKJV

They were supposed to rejoice because the joy of the "Lord was their strength, in Philippians it says,

"Rejoice in the "Lord always. Again, I will say, rejoice!"

Philippians 4:4 NKJV

Paul wants us to know as a believer in Jesus Christ that our "secret is prayer but the source of power is joy". The word of God is supposed to bring you joy in John it confirms this by saying,

"And these things we write to you that your joy may be full."

I John 1:4 NKJV

God wants you to enjoy reading the bible! In book of Nehemiah, they were obeying the law that had been read to them and their response was with Great Joy!

The word revival means "to recover life", which is a," restoration to bodily or mental vigor to life or consciousness".

"For to this end Christ died and rose and lived again, that He might be "Lord of both the dead and the living."

Romans 14:9 NKJV

The word revival when talking to born again believers, refers to the believer in Christ that were in a poor spiritual state, who were brought back to vitality and power. The word revival is also use when an unbeliever becomes a born-again believer in Christ.

"Therefore, if anyone is in Christ, he is a new creation; old things have passed away; behold, all things have become new."

II Corinthians 5:17 NKJV

To continue to have great massive and effective soul-winning results, we need to see and hear about people being revive daily. In this chapter we will see how a certain time period revival followed the reading of the word of God. Ezra read from the pulpit by the water gate. Having never heard the word of God before they cried. The word of God had a tremendous effect on the people they recognize how far short they had fallen from the standard God had set for them, there cannot be any revival without the teaching and preaching of the word of God.

"For all have sinned and fall short of the glory of God,"

Romans 3:23 NKJV

We have all have sinned and fallen short, but the word of God has revived us, Praise God!

"If we say that we have no sin, we deceive ourselves, and the truth is not in us. If we confess our sins, He is faithful and just to forgive us our sins and to cleanse us from all unrighteousness."

I John 1:8-9 NKJV

When you read the word of God you will come to the realization that either you are a sinner and or you have fallen short. The word confession means to agree with God's word instead of offering excuses or attempting to rationalize our actions. Confession is calling what you are doing or thinking exactly what it is, which is sin. Once you've confessed your sins, God is faithful and just to forgive you of your sins. Don't attempt to serve God when you are not trying to obedient to his word.

"But be doers of the word, and not hearers only, deceiving yourselves."

James 1:22 NKJV

"If we say that we have fellowship with Him, and walk in darkness, we lie and do not practice the truth. But if we walk in the light as He is in the light, we have fellowship with one another, and the blood of Jesus Christ His Son cleanses us from all sin. If we say that we have no sin, we deceive ourselves, and the truth is not in us. If we confess our sins, He is faithful and just to forgive us our sins and to cleanse us from all unrighteousness. If we say that we have not sinned, we make Him a liar, and His word is not in us."

I John 1:6-10 NKJV

In chapter ten it talks about how the Israelites are making a covenant with God. Have you ever made a Covenant with God?

The people were willing to do anything that God wanted them to do. The people cast lots and one out of every ten would stay in Jerusalem, the other nine would move to other cities. Everyone that was willing to stay in Jerusalem names were listed. Chapter twelve continues the list that was started in chapter eleven of the people that praise God. This chapter is also devoted to a dedication of the walls of Jerusalem. Nehemiah brought people from all over the land to this dedication because Jerusalem was the city where the temple was. The strangers, visitors and others passing through that land who heard great praise was wondering what was going on. Somewhere between chapter twelve and thirteen Nehemiah return to his job in the palace at Shushan. Remember, he had only asked for a leave of absence. He had been back in Persia for no more than two years when he had asked for another leave of absence so that he could go to Jerusalem. After the reading the Israelites decided to be obedient to the word of God. They had intermarried with Ammonites and Moabites, which God had forbidden. The children of Israel realized they must put them out of the land. Eliashib the high priest, through the marriage of his son or daughter, allied to the house of Tobiah. The high priest himself had disobeyed God in this important matter of separation. God had strictly forbidden intermarriage with the heathen. The priest had turned over the temple storage room to

Tobiah. They no longer brought the offerings of the people to the storage place. While Nehemiah was away, He decided to move Tobiah out of the chamber. Nehemiah had the chamber cleaned so the rooms would be put back into order for their original purpose in the service of God. Nehemiah didn't stop there. The Levites who served in the temple had not been properly supported; so, they had to get a job working in the fields. Gods' services had been neglected. Just before the sabbath, at sunset, Nehemiah commanded that the gates be shut. The merchants came with their wares thinking they could sell them. Nehemiah crawled up on the wall to see if the merchants had come, and they were waiting outside the gates. They came on the first Sabbath that the gates were closed, and they came on the second Sabbath and the gates were closed. Then Nehemiah told them, "If you come again, I will lay hands on you." and notice the scripture ended with "they came no more on the sabbath. Nehemiah discovers Jews who had married a woman from the nations. Nehemiah "contended with them, cursed them, smote certain of them and plucked off their hair! When it says that he "cursed" them, it doesn't mean that he swore at them, but that he pronounces a curse upon them, and he made them swear that they would not continue to intermarry with foreigners. He was using extreme measures, but they were needed. Now, Nehemiah brings the book and chapter to a close by talking about his great contributions to the spiritual wellbeing of his people. All foreigners were removed from positions of honor and responsibility, and the priest and Levites were given back their proper occupations. The offerings for the temple were resume. Nehemiah's final words were, "Remember me, O my God, for good! Nehemiah was a great layman!

The Nehemiah Plan

3 So I sent messengers to them, saying, "I am doing a great work and cannot come down. Why should the work stop while I leave to come down to [meet with] you?"

Nehemiah 6:3 AMP

Prepare yourself:

- Mourn the condition of people and the city, fast and pray

4 So it was, when I heard these words, that I sat down and wept, and mourned for many days; I was fasting and praying before the God of heaven.

Nehemiah 1:4 NKJV

- Remember Gods Covenant with his people and the importance of obedience and love

5 And I said: "I pray, "LORD God of heaven, O great and awesome God, you who keep Your covenant and mercy with those who love You and observe Your commandments,

Nehemiah 1:5 NKJV

- Confess sin, both personal and corporate

6 please let Your ear be attentive and Your eyes open, that You may hear the prayer of Your servant which I pray before You now, day and night, for the children of Israel Your servants, and confess the sins of the children of Israel which we have sinned against You. Both my father's house and I have sinned.

Nehemiah 1:6 NKJV

- Acknowledge a pre-condition of repentance and obedience in order to be gathered under God

9 but if you return to Me, and keep My commandments and do them, though some of you were cast out to the farthest part of the heavens, yet I will gather them from there, and bring them to the place which I have chosen as a dwelling for My name.'

Nehemiah 1:9 NKJV

Mobilize your resources:

- Pray for favor from those in authority.

11 O "Lord, I pray, please let Your ear be attentive to the prayer of Your servant, and to the prayer of Your servants who desire to fear Your name; and let Your servant prosper this day, I pray, and grant him mercy in the sight of this man."

Nehemiah 1:11 NKJV

- Speak clearly about the need and the plan to rebuild

3 and said to the king, "May the king live forever! Why should my face not be sad, when the city, the place of my fathers' tombs, lies waste, and its gates are burned with fire?"4 Then the king said to me, "What do you request?" So, I prayed to the God of heaven. 5 And I said to the king, "If it pleases the king, and if your servant has found favor in your sight, I ask that you send me

Nehemiah 2:3-5 NKJV

- Obtain letters of authorization and endorsement

7 Furthermore I said to the king, "If it pleases the king, let letters be given to me for the governors of the region beyond the river, that they must permit me to pass through till I come to Judah,

Nehemiah 2:7 NKJV

- Expect resistance from the enemy

10 When Sanballat the Horonite and Tobiah the Ammonite official heard of it, they were deeply disturbed that a man had come to seek the well-being of the children of Israel.

Nehemiah 2:10 NKJV

- Inspect and understand the city

11 So I came to Jerusalem and was there three days. 12 Then I arose in the night, I and a few men with me; I

told no one what my God had put in my heart to do at Jerusalem; nor was there any animal with me, except the one on which I rode. 13 And I went out by night through the Valley Gate to the Serpent Well and the Refuse Gate and viewed the walls of Jerusalem which were broken down and its gates which were burned with fire. 14 Then I went on to the Fountain Gate and to the King's Pool, but there was no room for the animal under me to pass. 15 So I went up in the night by the valley and viewed the wall; then I turned back and entered by the Valley Gate, and so returned. 16 And the officials did not know where I had gone or what I had done; I had not yet told the Jews, the priests, the nobles, the officials, or the others who did the work.

Nehemiah 2:11-16 NKJV

- Develop a leadership coalition who keeps a view of the whole

17 Then I said to them, "You see the distress that we are in, how Jerusalem lies waste, and its gates are burned with fire. Come and let us build the wall of Jerusalem, that we may no longer be a reproach." 18 And I told them of the hand of my God which had been good upon me, and also, of the king's words that he had spoken to me. So, they said, "Let us rise up and build." Then they set their hands to this good work.

Nehemiah 2:17-18 NKJV

- Continue to pray for protection from the enemy

8 and all of them conspired together to come and attack Jerusalem and create confusion. 9 Nevertheless we made our prayer to our God, and because of them we set a watch against them day and night.

Nehemiah 4:8-9 NKJV

Get to work on specific projects

- Some will work on their portion of the wall; others will address features that are needed or valuable for all (the gates). Organize teams to work on specific projects

3 Then Eliashib the high priest rose up with his brethren the priests and built the Sheep Gate; they consecrated it and hung its doors. They built as far as the Tower of the Hundred, *and* consecrated it, then as far as the Tower of Hananel. 2 Next to *Eliashib* the men of Jericho built. And next to them Zaccur the son of Imri built. 3 Also the sons of Hassenaah built the Fish Gate; they laid its beams and hung its doors with its bolts and bars. 4 And next to them Meremoth the son of Urijah, the son of]Koz, made repairs. Next to them Meshullam the son of Berechiah, the son of Meshezabel, made repairs. Next to them Zadok the son of Baana made repairs. 5 Next to them the Tekoites made repairs; but their nobles did not put their shoulders to the work of their Lord. 6 Moreover Jehoiada the son of Paseah and Meshullam the son of Besodeiah repaired the Old Gate; they laid its beams and hung its doors, with its bolts and bars. 7 And next to them Melatiah the Gibeonite, Jadon the

Meronothite, the men of Gibeon and Mizpah, repaired
the residence of the governor *of the region* beyond the
River. [8] Next to him Uzziel the son of Harhaiah, one of the
goldsmiths, made repairs. Also next to him Hananiah,
one of the perfumers, made repairs; and they fortified
Jerusalem as far as the Broad Wall. [9] And next to them
Rephaiah the son of Hur, leader of half the district of
Jerusalem, made repairs. [10] Next to them Jedaiah the son
of Harumaph made repairs in front of his house. And
next to him Hattush the son of Hashabniah made repairs.
[11] Malchijah the son of Harim and Hashub the son of
Pahath-Moab repaired another section, as well as the
Tower of the Ovens. [12] And next to him was Shallum the
son of Hallohesh, leader of half the district of Jerusalem;
he and his daughters made repairs. [13] Hanun and the
inhabitants of Zanoah repaired the Valley Gate. They
built it, hung its doors with its bolts and bars, and
repaired a thousand cubits of the wall as far as the
Refuse Gate. [14] Malchijah the son of Rechab, leader of the
district of Beth Haccerem, repaired the Refuse Gate; he
built it and hung its doors with its bolts and bars. [15]
Shallun the son of Col-Hozeh, leader of the district of
Mizpah, repaired the Fountain Gate; he built it, covered
it, hung its doors with its bolts and bars, and repaired
the wall of the Pool of Shelah by the King's Garden, as far
as the stairs that go down from the City of David. [16] After
him Nehemiah the son of Azbuk, leader of half the
district of Beth Zur, made repairs as far as *the place* in
front of the tombs of David, to the man-made pool, and
as far as the House of the Mighty.

17 After him the Levites, *under* Rehum the son of Bani, made repairs. Next to him Hashabiah, leader of half the district of Keilah, made repairs for his district. 18 After him their brethren, *under* Bavai the son of Henadad, leader of the *other* half of the district of Keilah, made repairs. 19 And next to him Ezer the son of Jeshua, the leader of Mizpah, repaired another section in front of the Ascent to the Armory at the buttress. 20 After him Baruch the son of Zabbai carefully repaired the other section, from the buttress to the door of the house of Eliashib the high priest. 21 After him Meremoth the son of Urijah, the son of Koz, repaired another section, from the door of the house of Eliashib to the end of the house of Eliashib. 22 And after him the priests, the men of the plain, made repairs. 23 After him Benjamin and Hasshub made repairs opposite their house. After them Azariah the son of Maaseiah, the son of Ananiah, made repairs by his house. 24 After him Binnui the son of Henadad repaired another section, from the house of Azariah to the buttress, even as far as the corner. 25 Palal the son of Uzai *made repairs* opposite the buttress, and on the tower which projects from the king's upper house that *was* by the court of the prison. After him Pedaiah the son of Parosh *made repairs.* 26 Moreover the Nethinim who dwelt in Ophel *made repairs* as far as *the place* in front of the Water Gate toward the east, and on the projecting tower. 27 After them the Tekoites repaired another section, next to the great projecting tower, and as far as the wall of Ophel.

28 Beyond the Horse Gate the priests made repairs,
each in front of his *own* house. 29 After them Zadok the
son of Immer made repairs in front of his *own* house.
After him Shemaiah the son of Shechaniah, the keeper of
the East Gate, made repairs. 30 After him Hananiah the
son of Shelemiah, and Hanun, the sixth son of Zalaph,
repaired another section. After him Meshullam the son
of Berechiah made repairs in front of his [r]dwelling. 31
After him Malchijah, [s]one of the goldsmiths, made
repairs as far as the house of the Nethinim and of the
merchants, in front of the Miphkad Gate, and as far as the
upper room at the corner. 32 And between the upper
room at the corner, as far as the Sheep Gate, the
goldsmiths and the merchants made repairs.

Nehemiah 3:1-32 NKJV

- Expect trouble and difficulty to dishearten those who labor in the effort

10 Then Judah said, "The strength of the laborers is
failing, and there is so much rubbish that we are not able
to build the wall." 11 And our adversaries said, "They
will neither know nor see anything, till we come into
their midst and kill them and cause the work to cease."
12 So it was, when the Jews who dwelt near them came,
that they told us ten times, "From whatever place you
turn, they will be upon us."

Nehemiah 4:10-12 NKJV

- Continually remind them of God's power and what you are fighting for

14 And I looked, and arose and said to the nobles, to the leaders, and to the rest of the people, "Do not be afraid of them. Remember the "Lord, great and awesome, and fight for your brethren, your sons, your daughters, your wives, and your houses."

Nehemiah 4:14 NKJV

- Create a separate initiative for protection at least half of the people involved should be focused on protection

16 So it was, from that time on, that half of my servants worked at construction, while the other half held the spears, the shields, the bows, and wore armor; and the leaders were behind all the house of Judah.

Nehemiah 4:16 NKJV

- Even the workers must be alert against the enemy and pray for each other

17 Those who built on the wall, and those who carried burdens, loaded themselves so that with one hand they worked at construction, and with the other held a weapon.

Nehemiah 4:17 NKJV

- Come to each other's aid when trouble comes and trust God for the fighting

20 Wherever you hear the sound of the trumpet, rally to us there. Our God will fight for us."

Nehemiah 4:20 NKJV

- Stay to the task, around the clock

22 At the same time I also said to the people, "Let each man and his servant stay at night in Jerusalem, that they may be our guard by night and a working party by day." 23 So neither I, my brethren, my servants, nor the men of the guard who followed me took off our clothes, except that everyone took them off for washing.

Nehemiah 4:22-23 NKJV

Message to the leaders

- The work requires capital and support, raise from the people, priest and officials. Acknowledge injustice. Call for support in the form of "repayment". Change the system of injustice. Praise God as people respond.

9 Then I said, "What you are doing is not good. Should you not walk in the fear of our God because of the reproach of the nations, our enemies? 10 I also, with my brethren and my servants, am lending them money and grain. Please, let us stop this usury! 11 Restore now to them, even this day, their lands, their vineyards, their olive groves, and their houses, also a hundredth of the money and the grain, the new wine and the oil, that you have charged them." 12 So they said, "We will restore it, and will require nothing from them; we will do as you

say." Then I called the priests and required an oath from them that they would do according to this promise. 13 Then I shook out the fold of my garment and said, "So may God shake out each man from his house, and from his property, who does not perform this promise. Even thus may he be shaken out and emptied." And all the assembly said, "Amen!" and praised the "LORD. Then the people did according to this promise.

Nehemiah 5:9-13 NKJV

- Leaders, serve alongside of the workers

15 But the former governors who were before me laid burdens on the people, and took from them bread and wine, besides forty shekels of silver. Yes, even their servants bore rule over the people, but I did not do so, because of the fear of God. 16 Indeed, I also continued the work on this wall, and we did not buy any land. All my servants were gathered there for the work.

Nehemiah 5:15-16 NKJV

- Keep a clear head, be alert, stay to the task, know the enemy's tricks, continue to pray

2 that Sanballat and Geshem sent to me, saying, "Come, let us meet together among the villages in the plain of Ono." But they thought to do me harm. 3 So I sent messengers to them, saying, "I am doing a great work, so that I cannot come down. Why should the work cease while I leave it and go down to you?" 4 But they sent me this message four times, and I answered them in

the same manner. 5 Then Sanballat sent his servant to me as before, the fifth time, with an open letter in his hand. 6 In it was written: It is reported among the nations, and Geshem says, that you and the Jews plan to rebel; therefore, according to these rumors, you are rebuilding the wall, that you may be their king. 7 And you have also appointed prophets to proclaim concerning you at Jerusalem, saying, "There is a king in Judah!" Now these matters will be reported to the king. So come, therefore, and let us consult together. 8 Then I sent to him, saying, "No such things as you say are being done, but you invent them in your own heart." 9 For they all were trying to make us afraid, saying, "Their hands will be weakened in the work, and it will not be done." Now therefore, O God, strengthen my hands.

Nehemiah 6:2-9 NKJV

- Be discerning of advisors, some are not from God

12 Then I perceived that God had not sent him at all, but that he pronounced this prophecy against me because Tobiah and Sanballat had hired him.

Nehemiah 6:12 NKJV

- Guard your reputation or you will sin and be discredited by the enemy to hinder your work

13 For this reason he was hired, that I should be afraid and act that way and sin, so that they might have cause for an evil report, that they might reproach me.

Nehemiah 6:13 NKJV

- Success is only possible with God's help, even the enemy knows that and when he sees it, he will be disheartened

16 And it happened, when all our enemies heard of it, and all the nations around us saw these things, that they were very disheartened in their own eyes; for they perceived that this work was done by our God.

Nehemiah 6:16 NKJV

- Know your people, catalog your assets and numbers

66 Altogether the whole assembly was forty-two thousand three hundred and sixty, 67 besides their male and female servants, of whom there were seven thousand three hundred and thirty-seven; and they had two hundred and forty-five men and women singers. 68 Their horses were seven hundred and thirty-six, their mules two hundred and forty-five, 69 their camels four hundred and thirty-five, and donkeys six thousand seven hundred and twenty.

Nehemiah 7:66-69 NKJV

- The heads of families will provide support

70 And some of the heads of the fathers' houses gave to the work. The governor gave to the treasury one thousand gold drachmas, fifty basins, and five hundred and thirty priestly garments.

Nehemiah 7:70 NKJV

Message to all who labor

- Celebrate together

9 And Nehemiah, who was the governor, Ezra the priest and scribe, and the Levites who instructed the people said to all the people, "This day is holy to the "LORD your God; do not mourn nor weep." For all the people wept, when they heard the words of the Law. 10
Then he said to them, "Go your way, eat the fat, drink the sweet, and send portions to those for whom nothing is prepared; for this day is holy to our "Lord. Do not sorrow, for the joy of the "LORD is your strength." 11 So
the Levites quieted all the people, saying, "Be still, for the day is holy; do not be grieved." 12 And all the people
went their way to eat and drink, to send portions and rejoice greatly, because they understood the words that were declared to them.

Nehemiah 8:9-12 NKJV

- Be nourished by God's word, daily

18 Also day by day, from the first day until the last day, he read from the Book of the Law of God. And they kept the feast seven days; and on the eighth day there was a sacred assembly, according to the prescribed manner.

Nehemiah 8:18 NKJV

- Fast, pray and confess sins together

9 Now on the twenty-fourth day of this month the children of Israel were assembled with fasting, in sackcloth, and with dust on their heads. 2 Then those of Israelite lineage separated themselves from all foreigners; and they stood and confessed their sins and the iniquities of their fathers. 3 And they stood up in their place and read from the Book of the Law of the "LORD their God for one-fourth of the day; and for another fourth they confessed and worshiped the "LORD their God.

Nehemiah 9:1-3 NKJV

- Remember God's mighty works

5 And the Levites, Jeshua, Kadmiel, Bani, Hashabniah, Sherebiah, Hodijah, Shebaniah, and Pethahiah, said: "Stand up and bless the "LORD your God Forever and ever! "Blessed be Your glorious name, which is exalted above all, blessing and praise! You alone are the "LORD; You have made heaven, The heaven of heavens, with all their host, The earth and everything on it, The seas and all that is in them, And You preserve them all. The host of heaven worships You. 7 "You are the "LORD God, Who chose Abram, And brought him out of Ur of the Chaldeans, And gave him the name Abraham; 8 You found his heart faithful before You, And made a covenant with him To give the land of the Canaanites, The Hittites, the Amorites, The Perizzites, the Jebusites, And the Girgashites— To give it to his descendants. You

have performed Your words, For You are righteous. 9 "You saw the affliction of our fathers in Egypt, And heard their cry by the Red Sea. 10 You showed signs and wonders against Pharaoh, Against all his servants, And against all the people of his land. For You knew that they acted proudly against them. So You made a name for Yourself, as it is this day. 11 And You divided the sea before them, So that they went through the midst of the sea on the dry land; And their persecutors You threw into the deep, As a stone into the mighty waters. 12 Moreover You led them by day with a cloudy pillar, And by night with a pillar of fire, To give them light on the road Which they should travel. 13 "You came down also on Mount Sinai, And spoke with them from heaven, And gave them just ordinances and true laws, Good statutes and commandments. 14 You made known to them Your holy Sabbath, And commanded them precepts, statutes and laws, By the hand of Moses Your servant. 15 You gave them bread from heaven for their hunger, And brought them water out of the rock for their thirst, And told them to go in to possess the land Which You had sworn to give them.

Nehemiah 9:5-15 NKJV

- Remember your weakness and failure to follow God in obedience

16 "But they and our fathers acted proudly, hardened their necks, and did not heed Your commandments.

Nehemiah 9:16 NKJV

- Remember how soon we forget our dependence on God and remember, that leads to losing everything!

"But after they had rest, they again did evil before You. Therefore, you left them in the hand of their enemies, so that they had dominion over them; Yet when they returned and cried out to You, you heard from heaven; And many times, you delivered them according to Your mercies,

Nehemiah 9:28 NKJV

- Commit together to be obedient

29 these joined with their brethren, their nobles, and entered into a curse and an oath to walk in God's Law, which was given by Moses the servant of God, and to observe and do all the commandments of the "LORD our "Lord, and His ordinances and His statutes:

Nehemiah 10:29 NKJV

CHAPTER 4

OUTREACH MARKETING

Outreach marketing is the process involved in promoting, selling in distributing a product, which is the management process through which goods and services move from concept to customer. It includes the coordination of four elements which are known as the four "P's" of marketing. Which are as follows,

Identification, selection, and development of a product

Determination of its price

Selection of a distribution channel to reach the customer's place

Development and implementation of a promotional strategy

Marketing is using your outreach program as a base to extend a hand, uplift and fulfill a void in someone's life. Whenever you're using your outreach tools as marketing and not selling you will always have a greater return because you are teaching people how to fish and not just giving them a fish, which means that they are not just being delivered from selling but they are being developed through outreach marketing. Selling always come with a trick and or technique of getting someone to exchange something such as cash for product, it can care less about the value of the product which is the person.

Outreach marketing is developing and creating a demand to introduce a product for cash or to someone that might not feel valued and help them to become valuable by supplying and fulfilling their needs not just for a day, but eternity.

The purpose for implementing a solid foundation for outreach marketing is not just to be affective, but to be effective. Even though the words affective and effective sound just alike they have two different meanings. The root word for "affective" is the root word "affect" and it is commonly used as a verb which means to influence an individual or group of people to have them feel, think, or act in a certain way. So, to be effective is therefore one of the most important characteristics that every outreach organization should possess to be successful in outreach marketing. The root word for "effective: is the word "effect" in contrast to the word *affect*, the word *effect* is used both as a noun and verb. As a noun the word effect generally means; The result of something; For something to be an *effect*, something else should have happened first. As a verb the word *effect* means; "the ability to produce the desired result" of the thing or person that is being affective.

So let's now bring these two words together so that you or your church, ministry or business will not just be affective but effective in all of your outreach marketing efforts.

To be an effective person, church, ministry or business effectiveness means that you have the ability to influence another person fillings, in way of thinking, for them to act and feel a certain way but an effective person is able to produce results, without first influencing another person's emotions in order to produce desired results just because you are an effective speaker does not mean that you are an effective outreach leader. Over the years I have seen many great preachers that are effective behind the pulpit and the brick and mortar of the building, there word delivery will have you jumping and shouting across the sanctuary but in front of the pulpit and beyond the walls of the brick and mortar the same preachers are not very effective at all because even though emotions were going on in the building, outside of the building no one was able to produce results.

Too many times I have asked people that were leaving out of a church service, "what was the word today? Their response was "I don't know but we sure did have some church today" there is a difference from having church and being the church. Having church, is working on your emotions to make you feel, think, or act a certain way, which is affective but being the church is taking your affectiveness and marrying to your effectiveness so that you can produce eternal results.

When you don't allow your affectiveness to be connected to your effectiveness you will always cause your organization to be ineffective, Which means it will be lacking in power and the ability or skill to perform effective outreach marketing.

Now that you understand the difference between these two words let's get back to why outreach marketing is so important one of the first reasons are; Because programs and giveaways can be done in a very informal and different type of settings which will encourage more people to show up to events of different ethnicities, ages and belief systems. The people that are staffing the outreach are mainly, if not all volunteers who are serving their community, city and state not because they have to do it in order to make a living which is; To clock in and clock out, but they are serving because they are driven by their passion to give and not take, this type of person realizes that in order for them to live a successful spiritual, physical and financial life they rely on the promise that was given to them from the foundations of the earth and delivered from their mother's womb. The day you were physically born from your mother's womb or the day a spiritual transformation took place in your mind, you probably ask yourself a question what was I created for to do on this earth?

One thing I want you to always remember is that " the promise of your prosperity is always connected to your passion".Let's take a look at five different types of outreaches, which are;

PUBLIC RELATION OUTREACH

DOMICILIARY OUTREACH

DETACHED OUTREACH

PERIPATETIC OUTREACH

SATELLITE OUTREACH

1. Public relation outreach: Public relations is a form of outreach but outreach itself is used to fill in the gap that mainstream services cannot provide which in return causes and effective outreach program to have good public relations throughout their community, city and state. The majority of people would rather not give to an overhead expense, but they will give to a program expense, which means that they are vicariously able to touch more people through someone else and at the same time their financial support has created a currency effect as it continues to flow throughout thousands of individuals on the earth.
2. Domiciliary Outreach: Is to provide care at someone domicile which is there permanent and legal residents and place of habitation where they are unable to take care of themselves because of age or disability and in need of someone to assist them.

3. Detached Outreach: This type of outreach is performed in a public environment, and it is an activity of providing services to disadvantaged individuals and families throughout the local community, city and state who would not normally receive the basics essentials for everyday living. These individuals can be in one of three categories if not all which are homeless, hopeless or helpless. For any organization to have a successful detached outreach program you cannot be stationary you have to be mobile and be willing to find the need and fill it, this cannot be done by waiting for them to come to you, but you have to go to where they are.
4. Peripatetic Outreach: This type of outreach can be performed in public or private environments, but it is different from detached outreach we're only certain individuals are targeted. Peripatetic outreach purpose is to target organizations only.
5. Dedicated Site Outreach: Outreach services are dedicated to only one site not multiple sites, such as; apartment buildings, nursing homes, public or private schools, city parks, streets, parking lots or any similar place that is a set place where you're church, ministry or business outreach marketing can be effective.

If you desire for your outreach marketing to be successful, you're going to have to stay motivated. The church is not just an Organism that is growing but it is also an organization. What is an organization? It is made-up of distinct units including doors, windows, roof etc. the floors of the building may be removed and replaced without destroying the integrity of the building but an Organism which is the human body does not allow you to remove an eye, ear, arm, foot, fingernail or tooth without destroying the integrity of the body without causing a mutilation to the body.

Your church, ministry or business needs to be marketed because of the great product it has to offer, which is providing help to disadvantaged individuals spiritually and physically. It's time for you to "get out of your seat and on your feet and in the "and start colliding with people throughout your community, city and state that need your services. Don't just be a collision in someone's life but have a great impact through their life. Stop being just a hearer and a talker and become a doer, why? Because someone is waiting for your obedience of activating your assignment that you have been given for to do in life. If you continue to walk around and try to be everyone else and do their assignment, then who is going to accomplish your God given assignment? You are the only you that has ever existed and there has never been another you before you and there will not be another you after you. So why would you try to be a copy when you are already the original? Have you ever asked God to bless and activity that you were doing and it seemed like that things were not coming together no matter how hard you were trying but instead of stopping the activity you kept on going, which consistently cause you to dig a hole of frustration within yourself which also inadvertently affected the people that are around you I wonder what would happen if you would stop asking God to bless what you're doing and start to do what he has already blessed? Remember that he is not just moved by your needs he is ultimately moved by your faith. Progress it's always before results!

SIX KEY PRINCIPLES TOWARD EFFECTIVE RESULTS

1. When you are quiet you can listen effectively.
2. When you are listening effectively you can remember.
3. When you are remembering you will have a better understanding.
4. When your understanding is clear you will always make good judgment.
5. When your judgment regarding a situation is understood it will be followed by your actions.
6. When your actions are activated, results follow.

Today is your day to stop looking like the chosen frozen and start to market the product or help the person that you have been assigned to. Stop being distracted by the enemy and stop fighting over man made denominations and dogmatic doctrines, remember that the most important thing is to reach, teach and watch the transformation change of an individual's life. Too much time is being spent discussing about denominations, doctrines, and organizations strategies, while tens of thousands of people are yelling for someone to come out and help. Even though your numerators might be different from others, your denominators can be the same which is to help people. To grow your church, ministry or business numerically you have to be consistent in saturating the marketplace.

When a person decides that they want to change the direction of their life from negative thinking to positive thinking, purchasing an item, prayer, or assistance with something, the first place they should think about going for assistance is to your church, ministry, or business. Let me ask you a question if I said to you, what is the first thing that comes to your mind when you think about French fries and a happy meal, what would be your answer? Come on, let's say it together, “McDonald's” even if you don't like the French fries at McDonald's the organization has saturated your mind with their product through consistent advertisement with outreach marketing, whenever you think about “happy meals” you will always think McDonald's.

Just like McDonald's presented their happy meals through outreach marketing you can do the same if you are willing to be specific and consistent in everything that you do. If you will continue to plant and water what you have planted you will eventually see an increase within your church, ministry, or business as a result of your labor. The issue is never about a harvest, but the issue is always about the labor. Without labor (Volunteers) it will always present a problem throughout your church, ministry or business causing stagnation which means that there is no movement at all. Remember, that marketing is not just designed to grow your church, ministry, or business but ultimately it is designed to expose your church, ministry, or business because what you don't "expose will never expand". Every successful church, ministry or business in the world has something to offer if they wholeheartedly believe in what they have been called and assigned to do. It amazes me how most if not all churches, ministries or businesses do not start doing evangelism, outreach or offering their product first in their own community and city before it's introduced to the world. When your evangelism and outreach efforts are done right it will introduce itself to the world, which now moves you from outreach social marketing to attraction outreach marketing. As I stated before if every church, ministry, or business would whole heartedly believe in what they have been assigned to do and just start talking about the good news of the gospel and how it will help disadvantaged individuals spiritually and physically their evangelism and outreach efforts will be effective.

Remember, "you can never promote a person or product successfully without having passion for the product that you are promoting."

BELIEVE-EXPECT-UNDERSTAND-TRUST

You must believe in the person or product that you are offering because if you don't who will.

You must expect that something great is going to happen with the person or product

You must understand the significance and value of who and what you're offering and how it will help another individual propel to their promotion and prosperity in life.

You must trust not just the creation of the product but the creator of the product.

For many years people I have been saying, "if you build it, they will come" and there is some truth to this but just because you built a big fish pond doesn't mean that all the fish are going to find their way to the pond unless you go get them and lead and/or place them in the pond. Even though there are many great preachers across America that have grown mega-churches, it is very important to remember that it's not the great preaching alone that grows mega-churches it is combined with "great leaders with aim focus leadership and great administration that causes a church to become mega-church". What's a mega-church? A mega-church is a church with an unusually large congregation, typically (not always) one preaching a conservative or form of Christianity. The question to be asked is, can you as a leader connect the people within your organization to your assignment that you have been given through vision casting? The reason why your vision, and assignment that you have been given is stagnant, because there is a lack of connecting others to what you, the church, ministry, or business have been assigned to do.

Outreach marketing is one of the major keys for growth in your church, ministry, or business. Most people who struggle in this area will never see or live the life that they have purposely been created for. Instead, they will always be frustrated with, not living a passionate purpose fulfilled life. One of the main reasons why you are not feeling fulfillment in life is not because of the blueprint or foundation that has been made and dug for you but because, the enemy wants to steal, kill and destroy your destiny that has been planned for you.

10 The thief comes only in order to steal and kill and destroy. I came that they may have *and* enjoy life, and have it in abundance [to the full, till it overflows].

John 10:10 AMP

If someone breaks into your house, car, or business it seems like they should be happy and satisfied with just stealing your merchandise, but their goal is to kill your dreams that has been planted in your heart. If you are going to grow your church, ministry, or business the first thing you must understand is that "exposure always creates expansion."

Can you imagine the tens of thousands of people that pass your church, ministry, or business location daily by walking, running, or driving, but never knew that you existed. If your church, ministry, or business closes its doors today, would the same people pass your old location and say to themselves and to everyone else, "what or do you know what used to be in that location"? Why does this happen? I have a very simple answer for you. There was no consistence outreach marketing in the community and city. That's why I have written and titled this book ""out of your seat on your feet and in the streets" to show you how your church, ministry or business can get the word out to let everyone know why your church, ministry or business exists.

I would like to introduce you to five family members known as the "Tator" family; each family has a different function in the family. You never know you could be part of one these families, see if you recognize which one you represent.

THE "TATOR" FAMILY

1.COMMENTATOR – This individual always asks, "What happen"? They rarely show up to the outreach events and when they are in attendance, they never do anything but talk.

2.SPECTATOR – This individual "always watch things happen", they always see the problems at every outreach event, but never provide an answer for the problem.

3.NON-PARTICPATOR – This individual "always let things happen", they are physically at outreach events but are mentally thinking about something else.

4.IRRITATOR – This individual represents all the above, they are always at the outreach events frustrating everyone and they are a huge liability instead of an asset.

5.PARTICIPATOR – This individual "makes things happen", they will always finish what they started at the outreach event.

In July of 1991 I started doing evangelism and outreach on the streets of Everett, Washington. I knew from the very beginning that I didn't want to be a person that would ask, watch, or let things happen and definitely not an irritator, that just complained all the time. I wanted to be a participator and make things happen. I wanted to allow the assignment that I have been created for to flow out of me, which was to empower people the be the best they can be, by first feeding them physically and then spiritually.

For over thirty-two years, I've continued to do this by teaching people how to "engage with others, be equipped and empowered for evangelism and outreach". The result of this teaching has motivated thousands of people across the United States and beyond to "get out of their seat on their feet and in the streets".

When I started to reach out to the homeless, hopeless and helpless which were people that were living on the streets experiencing food insecurity, I quickly realized that I didn't just want to preach to the people the corner of Colby and Hewitt, which is located in downtown Everett but rather give them something to eat and drink while I was preaching and teaching and maybe they will listen to what I have to say. Ask yourself a question is your church, ministry or business answering questions that nobody is asking, instead of answering questions that people are asking. Give the Hungry something to eat and maybe they might listen to what you have to say. Also, remember that some of your greatest business or ministry meetings took place where food was involved.

Make sure your outreach team is driven with the same passion and purpose that you have because your inner circle will either devalue your worth or raise your value this is known as regression and progression, for instance; if there are twenty houses in a community and the nice house is surrounded by nineteen bad houses, the nice house is now devalued because of the other houses in it's community but if there are twenty houses in a community and the bad house is surrounded by the nineteen nice houses the property value of the bad house is raised because of the twenty nice houses. Never let anyone tell you that it does not matter who you spend your time with because, bad company will always corrupt good manners and just because it might seem permissible for you to hang around this type of individual is probably not beneficial for you.

[33] Don't be fooled by those who say such things. If you listen to them you will start acting like them.

1 Corinthians 15:33 TLB

[23] All things are lawful [that is, morally legitimate, permissible], but not all things are beneficial *or* advantageous. All things are lawful, but not all things are constructive [to character] *and* edifying [to spiritual life].

1 Corinthians 10:23 AMP

I'm going to ask you again, if your church, ministry, or business close down today would people remember what was in that location or who you were? If you would like to have a great impact in your community or city, you first must have a collision with the people. The ultimate excitement does not start with the first time that people walk through the doors of your church, ministry or business, that is the beginning and not the ending but it's when they come back through the door two, three, or four more times, that should make you even more excited, because that means that they were being empowered by what you have to offer. So, two questions to ask yourself is, how can I get people to come to my church, ministry, or business? How can I improve the retention process? One thing vitally important to remember is that people will never come uninvited. In my book titled "Taking it to the Streets" in chapter three, I give multiple principles on how to invite people to church. Also, a ninety- day cycle that will grow a church of ten people to five hundred base on a 1%

return in only five years. Go to www.RayHampton.com or www.Amazon.com and order your book online today.

When you know what your purpose and position is in Christ only Jesus Christ himself can disqualify you. People's criticism of your assignment shouldn't never bother you because that's probably the only time that they thought about you, so stop worrying, being frustrated and stop trying to make them understand you. Your purpose did not come from them anyway it was impregnated in you by the Holy Spirit but needs to be cultivated and delivered by you. The assignment you were created for has never been done by anyone on this earth and that's why if you try to be someone else then, who is going to be you so why don't you just do you! Most people are satisfied just doing God's work and think they are completed in doing their assignment but just because you're doing God's work does not mean you are doing God's assignment for your life.

"You will never be defeated by what other people say about you, you are only defeated by what you say about yourself". Have you ever stopped to wonder why every time that you're getting close to a blessing or when God starts to do something amazing in your life false accusations begin to arise around you through friends, family and or business partners that you thought believe in you as well as your assignment that you have been called to do in life. If you've experienced this type of situation in your life, I have some great news for you "never stopped to answer your critics", "scandals only come out when you're in the finals". Be attentive to people that smile at your defeats all the time. People that smile and laugh at your defeats all the time is like a dog that only shows all their teeth, when he's preparing to bark at you or bite. The two most important things I want you to grasp through everything that I have already spoken to you previous is to "stay consistent in your outreach marketing efforts" and "failures in outreach events are not final". If you have failed in any of your evangelism and outreach efforts, never give up because F.A.I.L. means "First Attempt In Learning". Your failures are not the end of you doing another evangelism and outreach event because E.N.D. means "Effort Never Dies". If you're looking for partnerships to do an evangelism and outreach event and keep getting a "no" as an answer, remember, N.O. means "Next Opportunity". Whenever people ask you the question, "how is the evangelism and outreach ministry going? Your response is, it's still in progress and doing great! Its important to know that your mentality towards evangelism and outreach is your reality and "If you shift your mindset about how to do evangelism and outreach, you'll shift the results that you'll receive pertaining to the harvest of souls to the Kingdom".

Most people are chasing their purpose, but their purpose is what is pulling them into their destiny. The subtitle of my book titled, "Taking it to the Streets" says "A Passion for a Purpose" Why? Because I strongly believe that it's my passion that continues to push me and it's my purpose that is constantly pulling me through the Journey to my destiny. Prayer is always the foundation and the key to your success that will unlock the door of opportunities, toward your destiny and if the door does not open then it's not for you to walk through at that time. If the timing for an evangelism and outreach event is wrong, God will say "Slow". If the request that you have made to God for an evangelism and outreach event is wrong, He'll say "No". If you are totally wrong about doing the evangelism and outreach event He'll say "Grow". If the request you made to God about doing the evangelism and outreach event timing is right, He'll say "Go". So just continue to rest in the Lord and trust that he knows the right timing and he will give you a piece that were surpasses all understanding.

7 And the peace of God [that peace which reassures the heart, that peace] which transcends all understanding, [that peace which] stands guard over your hearts and your minds in Christ Jesus [is yours].

Philippians 4:7 AMP

The title of this book "out of your seat on your feet and in the streets" was written for the purpose to empower, encourage and enlighten you to stay mission minded by reaching one person at a time. You can make all the plans you want for your life but until you surrender your plans for the plan and purpose that has already been designed for you, you will never experience a fulfilled life of why you exist. Remember no one can stop God's plan for your life but you so you might as well just DO YOU! Because failure is never final.

Does your church, ministry or business have a strong outreach marketing strategy?

It doesn't matter if you're a profit or non- profit organization you are only effective when you have a strong marketing outreach strategy and be willing to be consistent and implement the strategic plan. Your outreach marketing strategy does not have to be expensive to be effective. A major key in developing a marketing outreach strategy is to form a solid foundation to enhance your promotional efforts. Promotional efforts include but not limited to, advertising, mailing and/or phone calling. Not to have an outreach marketing strategy it's like buying a a lot of furniture for a home you're thinking about building but don't know what the square footage is. How would you even know how much furniture to buy or what size to buy.

19 OUTREACH MARKETING FOCAL POINTS

1. You must stay focused
2. You cannot think any higher than the level you are expose to because exposure brings expansion.
3. Your success is in your difference from others what makes you unique from everyone else.
4. What do you dislike that motivates you?

5. Don't expect everyone to understand you because there has never been another you before you existed.
6. Practice does not just give you perfect results, but it will give you permanent results.
7. Competition is never against someone else it's only against yourself to be the best you.
8. If you try to become someone else, then who is supposed to be you.
9. What are you good at that will maximize your potential?
10. You must be in tune to the sound and rhythm of your assignment and calling for your life.
11. Change is only change when you change.
12. Preach the gospel and if necessary, use words.
13. Don't try to change the world but change your world.
14. Look for problems in your community where you can provide an answer.
15. Always serve with your palms down and not your palms up.
16. Don't live your life "tapping" people but live your life "touching" people.
17. People don't care how much you know until they know how much you care.

18. Know your identity.
19. If you try to reach the thousands you might not touch the one but, when you touch the one you will reach the thousands.

Remember to always focus on the "process more than the results" what is a process?" It is a series of actions or steps taken in order to achieve a particular end. There are many times in life that your own strength will not accomplish your assignments in life, but it is through Christ who gives you the ultimate strength to accomplish the assignment, that you have been assigned to do for your life. Remember, that since Jesus began the work in you, He's also the one that will complete the work through you. If you continue to stay with His plans for your life the rewards are great, and the daily benefits are loaded with blessings.

13 I can do all things [which He has called me to do] through Him who strengthens *and* empowers me [to fulfill His purpose—I am self-sufficient in Christ's sufficiency; I am ready for anything and equal to anything through Him who infuses me with inner strength and confident peace.]

Philippians 4:13 AMP

6 I am convinced *and* confident of this very thing, that He who has begun a good work in you will [continue to] perfect *and* complete it until the day of Christ Jesus [the time of His return].

Philippians 1:6

When you are focused on the assignment that God has called you to do in life, you can ignore the distractions or sounds around you which will allow you to only hear the voice of God's direction for your life. When God is not speaking it's a good idea for you to not make a move at all and just continue to rest in him. To rest doesn't mean for you to completely stop what you're doing but it does mean for you to continue what you are currently doing until He gives you the green light to move forward. Promotion just doesn't come from what you are doing it's received by what God is doing through you. Throughout the years, I've shared with thousands of people that success is, following the instructions that you have been given to do without asking God a lot of questions. I have spent a lot of personal time and money throughout my life trying to find someone that was doing the same type of outreach I had been called to do. There were organizations that were similar but not the same. I was like driving down a dead end street try to find someone doing the same assignment that was planted in my heart to do but as I search and served I was never became fulfilled, so I just did whatever they did, not that it was the wrong thing to do but ultimately it was not the right thing for me to do. Just because all things might be permissible to you does not mean they are beneficial for you.

One day something just landed in my thought process, and I came to the realization that if I kept trying to be everybody else then who was going to be me. Maybe what I was created for had not even been invented yet. Eventually I activated my measure of faith and did what I was created to do. Since I had already been delivered from a negative way of thinking I definitely did not want to go back to that way of thinking again because now i realize that, how an individual thinks they will eventually become, so I just stopped depending on my own knowledge and started to trust the one that not only gave me knowledge but can also at any time enhance the knowledge that he has already given me. Now once I started to listen and carry out my assignment throughout the nation that's when all the attacks began on and in my life but as always, I went to the source who is provider of all resources, where I always received a comforting word. I knew at that moment that my assignment was greater than the attacks that was trying to distract me and if I stayed in my lane I will never get into a wreck. There might be people in front of me that are going faster or people behind pushing me but as long as I stay in my lane, I knew I would continue to move forward on the path, in His plan, His promises and prosperity for my life, because I was committed to pushing toward my destiny.

The assignment that has been assigned to you for your life is not to compete against another individual but to complete them. You are not supposed to be in competition with others but only to encourage, empower or to be in covenant, especially when it comes to the outreach marketing of your church, ministry or business. I will be expounding more on this subject when I discuss the importance of partnership and networking.

In July 1991 as I was watching the 11:00 PM channel 7 news and hearing about people who were living on the streets that were homeless and hungry something within me was stirring up and at the very moment I knew that I was called to make a difference in another person's life through serving, to do this effectively I knew that I could not change the whole world, but I could change my world and once my world was changed everything that I was connected to would begin to change. After days, weeks and months continue to go by I continue to watch the news regarding the issues of the homeless and the hungry that continue to rise at an alarming rate and suddenly one day it was like I could her a school bell ringing in my spirit and at that very moment I knew that it was time to sound the alarm. I began to feel a shift within my spirit that something great as about to happen in my life. Being a solution to the problems that had risen on the streets regarding the homeless and hungry I started to provide an answer to the need. There are probably many times in your life that you might have had a good idea, but it might not necessarily had been a God idea. The difference between a good idea and a God idea is, good ideas is God permissive will, but God ideas is God's perfect will for your life, so I wanted to be in the perfect will of God. I didn't have a bachelor's degree, a master's degree, or doctoral degree, but I began to search the word of God for faith scriptures that pertain to what I had been steering in my heart and mind. I realized that since I was been born again I had actually already had my "bachelor's degree" and since I had been "touched by the master" I had my master's degree and last but not least I had a Ph.D. because I have the "power of the Holy Spirit and had been delivered" so if I just continue to trust the Lord with all my heart and lean not to my own understanding and acknowledge him that he would direct all of my steps and even though sometimes I might stumble I was still stepping. The great news is at the time of this writing I have accomplished my higher educational success by attending Washington State University and A.L. Hardy Academy of Theology. I received my bachelor's in theology, masters in marriage and biblical family counseling and two doctoral degrees in ministry and theology.

Why should you advertise or market your evangelism and outreach events? I'm going to ask you the following questions: Have you ever heard of McDonald's, Wendy's, Burger King, Kentucky fried chicken, jack-in-the-box, Taco Bell, Taco time, white castles, crystals, cracker barrel, Microsoft, or Amazon? My guess is that you have heard of at least one of these organizations if not all but none of these companies have to advertise with signage on buildings or property for you to know who they are, but the advertisement is, so you don't forget who they are.

Nike and Verizon don't advertise because you do not know who they are; Their goal is to convince you that going to any other company to buy products will not be of the same value. These companies have created a mental passage through your brain to make you think about a product that someone else sells that is similar to theirs you will always go to them because of their marketing strategy, they have implanted in your mind to think that their value of their product is always higher than everyone else this term is known as, "competitive advantage". You're probably wondering what is the definition for this term, competitive advantage is; a condition or circumstance that puts a company in a favorable or superior business position and expansion is vital to maintaining a competitive advantage as an organization, if your focus is on building people instead of building buildings you will not have a building big enough to contain all the people that you have empowered and equipped because you will be at capacity in your building which means that you would have to call for help to share the harvest this is what I call, "people over product".

When companies realize that their sales are down one of the first things that they do is increase their marketing spending for the next quarter. They understand that in order for revenue to increase, they must expose their problem for deeper penetration in the market. When your profit or non-profit organization is in a financial bind, the first thing that most leaders do is delete some if not all advertisement from the evangelism and outreach marketing budget. The very thing that is helping to expose the organization has now been deleted from the budget. Instead, they keep funding programs that are stagnant instead of realizing without people there are no programs. To help you with this process I have compiled in this book a chapter titled "Outreach Ideas" which I've listed almost two-hundred outreach marketing ideas to help you get started.

THE "NET" BROKE

5 So it was, as the multitude pressed about Him to
hear the word of God, that He stood by the Lake of
Gennesaret, 2 and saw two boats standing by the lake;
but the fishermen had gone from them and were
washing *their* nets. 3 Then He got into one of the boats,
which was Simon's, and asked him to put out a little from
the land. And He sat down and taught the multitudes
from the boat.

4 When He had stopped speaking, He said to Simon,
"Launch out into the deep and let down your nets for a
catch."

5 But Simon answered and said to Him, "Master, we
have toiled all night and caught nothing; nevertheless at
Your word I will let down the net." 6 And when they had
done this, they caught a great number of fish, and their
net was breaking. 7 So they signaled to *their* partners in
the other boat to come and help them. And they came
and filled both the boats, so that they began to sink. 8
When Simon Peter saw *it,* he fell down at Jesus' knees,
saying, "Depart from me, for I am a sinful man, O Lord!"

[9] For he and all who were with him were astonished at the catch of fish which they had taken; [10] and so also *were* James and John, the sons of Zebedee, who were partners with Simon. And Jesus said to Simon, "Do not be afraid. From now on you will catch men." [11] So when they had brought their boats to land, they forsook all and followed Him.

Luke 5:1-11 NKJV

POWER OF PARTNERSHIP

[6] I planted, Apollos watered, but God gave the increase.

1 Corinthians 3:6 NKJV

Two of the greatest enhancement to knowing how to market your outreach is first understanding what the meaning of the word's partnership and networking. Partnership can either take away or add value to your outreach marketing plans This is why being in unity and harmony with the individual or organization you are partnering with can make a big difference in not just your affectiveness but your effectiveness. You can always highlight the affectiveness of being out of tune, but you cannot hide the effectiveness of the rhythm of the organization. Affective describes something that has been influenced by emotions, is a result of emotions, or expresses emotion. Effective describes something that produces a desired result.

What is the meaning of the word plottage in real estate? "Plottage" is a term that refers to the increase in valuation realized when many smaller parcels of land are combined into a single larger parcel. The principle of plottage is the increase in value realized by combining adjacent parcels of land into one larger parcel. The process of combining the parcels is known as assemblage. Generally, the value of the whole parcel will be greater than the sum of the individual smaller parcels. As an organization you have a specific calling and once you hook up and connect with like-minded people that is going in the same direction that you are going you will always win every time. I highly recommend that you don't spend a lot of time always focusing on your losses but stay forward focus on the destination so you can arrive at the finish line. The right partnership in your life will always add value to whatever you're doing in return not just one person will win but everyone wins. The real question you might be wondering right now is what the meaning of the word partnership is; a partnership is an arrangement where two people or organizations agree to cooperate to advance their mutual interests. Since we are social beings, partnerships between individuals, business, interest-based organizations, schools, governments, and a variety of combinations will always remain a commonplace. A partnership is formed between one or more businesses in which partners Co-labor to achieve and share profit and losses. Partnership exists within and across non-profit and profit organizations that are partnering together to increase the likelihood of their outreach marketing to achieve their vision and mission. Partnership always starts at a personal level, such as when two or more individuals agree to domicile together. It is very dangerous for you to even consider connecting with another individual or organization that cannot enhance what you have been created to do, the bottom line is if it does not add value to your organization, it is subtracting away from it. Be very careful of individuals of organizations that are sponges in your life, which means they are soaking everything up from you and the organization but not giving anything back in return.

THE POWER OF "NET" WORKING

Just like partnership is powerful networking is just as powerful for your church, ministry, or business. The right partnership can add value to your church, ministry, or business but networking will always enhance the value that has been added. Several years ago, a powerful statement was downloaded into my spirit as I begin to network with other churches, ministries, and businesses, which was "if you're not networking, you're not working" and today I'm still quoting the same phrase. What is the definition of a net? A net can be and interlocking or intertwining of individuals who are related to one another through mutual contacts! Which means that one person is connected to another, who is directly connected to someone else, and it keeps on going. What is the definition of work? work is a common word but once it is connected to the word net it now becomes an action word, such as "net-work" which is a group or system of interconnected people or things; or a group of people who exchange information, contacts, and experiences for professional or social purpose. To have your network work effectively for your church, ministry, or business you must put in the work to get the results that you want, or it will never "worked if you don't work it" a lot of outreach organizations expect to receive something without putting in the work, but you have to stay connected to the source which causes your resources to flow. Now that we have looked at the word "net" and the word "work" now let's take a closer look at the last three letters of the word "Networking" which is "ING", which means "I" (Inviting) "N" (New) "G" (Guest). Now that you have extended your net you can expect your church, ministry, or business to grow. Now let's look at what the word networking means, networking is; to interact with other people to exchange information and develop contacts to extend their reach; or to use a contact made in business for the purpose beyond the reason for the initial contact. The real question is what does the networking mean to you? Over the years I've heard many people make statements such as, "I know so many people, but it never gets me anywhere "the problem with this statement it's not who you know but what and who they know that can make a tremendous difference in the value of the networking relationship. Maybe you're just hanging around too many people that have your problem, but they are not your answer. It's not always about the quantity of people that you know but it's also about the quality of people that you know. The following are three key questions that you might want to ask yourself when you're networking. "Am I more interested in the other person or am I just talking about myself", "Am I talking negative gossip or does my conversing in conversation add value to the other person", "Am I a liability or asset to this person "take a good look at your answers because you might see your problem in your outreach marketing efforts. If you continue to do the same thing the same negative way, you're always going to get the same negative results but if you change your thinking process positive things will happen. The mindset of a successful networker is to provide value to others and not just to always get business or help for themselves. For you to have a great outreach marketing organization you must gain the respect and trust of others which will often translate into success and credibility.

"The message is what's sacred not the method"

25Jesus, knowing their thoughts, called them to his side and said, "Kings and those with great authority in this world rule oppressively over their subjects, like tyrants. 26But this is not your calling. You will lead by a completely different model.

Matthew 20:25-26a TPT

11 KEY OUTREACH MARKETING POINTS A NETWORKER NEEDS

1. Are you authentic and true to your word.
2. Are you consistent in both what you say and do?
3. Do you lose focus in times of trouble, hardship, or temptation?
4. Are you passionate and speak from your heart while allowing your listener to speak and be heard as well.
5. Are you outgoing?
6. Are you sincere?
7. Are you friendly?
8. Are you supportive?
9. Are you a good listener?
10. Do you follow up and stay in touch with people?
11. Do you give other people referrals and ideas without thinking about your own personal gain.

If you would just apply the eleven preceding key points to your outreach marketing, you will experience success in everything you do. The ability to network is one of the most important tools in any outreach marketing plan because it will provide you the contacts that are necessary to grow your church, ministry, or business. Many people go to networking events but very few people know how to network effectively. Networking is more than just getting out and meeting people. Networking is a structure plan to get to know people who will do business with you or introduce you to other people who will do business with you. The best way to have continued success in your outreach efforts is to plan because "if you fail to plan, then you are planning to fail "commit to your plan no matter who says it's not going to work. Always remember "if you live by their complaints you will give up because of their criticism". Always be consistent in executing your plan in good or bad times.

Now that you have a plan it's very important that you stay committed to the plan as well as cultivate the plan. Fifty percent of successful networking is reaching out; therefore, it is called outreach marketing. To see the results of your networking efforts you can't stay within the four walls of the church, ministry, or business. Just because you attend several networking groups your church, ministry or business will never become successful if you continue to always meet with the same people, why? because you'll continue to get the same results. In networking you must be willing to expand your territory to receive continued growth. Another key to successful networking is to always be proactive so you do not become reactive causing you to be confused on what to do once you attend a networking event. To be proactive is creating or controlling a situation by causing something to happen rather than responding to it after it has happened. To be reactive is acting in response to a situation rather than creating or controlling it. Being proactive will prevent any potential problems and will save yourself a lot of heartache and stress.

SEVEN KEYS TO "NETWORKING"

Remember if you're not "networking" you're notworking.

1. Set a goal to meet a certain amount of people at every networking event that you attend.
2. Always look for people that you have never met and let it become a habit, if you don't you will always naturally gravitate toward people that you already know.
3. Attend multiple networking groups. This way you will not only expand your networking efforts you will also be able to find your niche. Always be willing to expose your church, ministry, or business because "what you don't expose will never expand ".
4. Carry your business cards with you all the time. You never know when you might relate to the current contact but if you don't have your cards with you, it is a guaranteed you will be disconnected from a future contact.

5. Stay active. When attending a networking event just don't go sit down in a chair you have to get involved in the inner workings of the group because it will always cause you to have great visibility throughout the group, remember that people are always looking for someone to be an "asset not a liability".
6. Be friendly and approachable always act like you're the host of any networking event that you attend, this will always cause people to feel welcome whenever they meet you and in return, they will always introduce you two other contacts as well. If you consistently stay focused on helping others soon you will find other people helping you.
7. Be willing to be a giver so you can be a receiver. Networking is a bilateral relationship don't expect new contacts if you're not willing to give any help.

Other terminologies for network marketing are social and attraction. Social marketing and attraction marketing are both network marketing tools. Social outreach marketing is the ability to reach out to potential and existing customers, using social media technology it helps everyone to interact with each other. Attraction outreach marketing is the ability for people to reach in as potential customers in searching out your church, ministry, or business. Remember, that "facts tell, and stories sell", your facts will always provide the proof and your stories will always tell the truth.

Some of the most successful people in networking are the ones that just don't talk about networking events, but they show up at the networking events. People that show up to these events are individuals that are committed to finding answers and are willing to do what it takes to solve their church, ministry, or business problems. As a leader it is very important that you get out of your comfort zone and go to the conferences that will empower and equip you to be the best you, it's totally up to you no one's going to make you do it, they only can suggest that you do it. You are the one that must make the move. When you become distracted trying to answer questions that no one is asking you are hindering your own personal knowledge which will affect your church, ministry, or business success. When you stop pursuing to network with others, your progress will slowdown, which will eventually limit your growth potential. It's very important for you to know when the light is red, yellow, or green.

SIX KEYS TO NET "NOT-WORKING"

Remember, if you're not networking, you're "not-working"

1. Afraid to go by yourself.

Most people that are starting nonprofit or profit organizations use this excuse all the time and if it is true, then they are a great candidate to go to the networking event. Because as we can see they need a friend!

2. Afraid to meet people.

I do understand that some people are very shy and uncomfortable at social events, but I want you to realize that you were made to be overcomer and a conqueror. You will never be able to "conquer what you don't confront". Have you wondered what would happen if you showed up to a networking event, that was packed to capacity of successful people that you have never met. This would be a great opportunity to you sit next to someone and engage in a conversation. You never know they might have the answer to your problem. You never know what people can do for you and what you can do for them unless you make a move. What great connections are you missing out on by not attending networking events? No successful student never passes their class by attending the class. It's vitally important that students attend their class no matter how they feel especially if they want to graduate to the next level.

3. Personal connections

Social media is an amazing and powerful tool for personal and business connections, but social media connections can never replace personal connections but what social media does offer is a connection with people that you probably never would've engage with. Once you meet a person on social media the power of connecting comes when you meet them face to face. You will never receive power for what your call to do until you get plugged in to the power source of networking, so "get out of your seat, on your feet and in the streets" and start making connections today.

4. You don't know it all.

Most people think they know everything about their business. Just because you have read books, attended a few conferences and have years of experience, don't ever think that there's nothing else for you to learn because once you "stop learning you will stop earning".

5. Stop and get some help!

Have you ever felt like that you have a lot to learn about how to network for your church, ministry, or business? Well, I have some great news for you stop feeling shame and embarrass and open your mouth and ask for help. Most people don't ask for help because they feel like they should be further along in their church, ministry or business or they believe it's a sign of showing weakness. If this is your attitude, I would like to drop some knowledge on you. All successful people get consistent help, most leaders, executives, pastors, managers, directors and so on has monthly mentors and committed coaching. It is vitally important that you get around people that have your answer and not your problem.

6. Stop worrying about who gets the credit.

Showing up to someone else's. event does not mean that it validates their success, but it might be just what you need to begin, enhance, or validate your own success. The truth is they are going to be successful whether you show up to the event or not. Don't let your insecurities hold you back from achieving your highest level of success.

Are you going to start doing what you have been assigned to do or are you going to keep making excuses why you can't do what your call to do? My advice to you is to not have a "stay in the boat mentality", and instead get out of the boat and don't let distractions detour you from your destiny.

CHAPTER 5

What is Digital and Non-Digital Footprint Marketing?

A digital footprint is the data that is left behind by users on a digital service. There are two main classifications for digital footprints: Passive and active. A passive digital footprint is created when data is collected without the owner knowing, whereas active digital footprints are created when personal data was released deliberately by user for the purpose of sharing information about oneself by means of websites or social media. A non-digital footprint is just the opposite it is not using the web at all, but it is your hand extended to someone else to know them physically and not just electronically. This type of marketing is known as traditional marketing because there is a paper trail of events that have been captured by word of mouth. The following ideas that are given is for you to think outside the box, Because I truly believe that God did not make you to be or remain in the box neither did, he just want you to be concerned about church work more than Kingdom work. Church work might be a "good idea" but Kingdom work is a "God idea" what is the major difference between these two ideas. A "good idea" is from yourself and the encouragement of other people that are connected or unconnected around you but a "God idea" is when God gives you a revelation that only he can reveal to you but if you refuse to accept and move on it you will miss the manifestation that God has for your life. Many people have gone out to do Kingdom work to try to increase their weekly local church attendance but when they didn't see any increase of people in the building they stop doing the work! Kingdom work takes a while to grow just because you don't see it right away doesn't mean it's not working. God makes all things grow!

6 I planted, Apollos watered, but God [all the while] was causing the growth.

1 Corinthians 3:6 AMP

Always think about new strategies for outreach ideas! When your strategies change your systems will change, which means; you will not have a stagnation of souls. Jesus came to empower people with the Gospel. Don't make it a habit in putting all your energy and resources into building a comfortable building with the hope that people will attend. As I travel across the United States, I'm consistently reminding people that, Jesus came to "comfort the afflicted, and to "afflict the comfortable". What is the meaning of the phrase to "comfort the afflicted and afflict the comfortable"? It is to provide aid or support to those in need, while prompting those in positions of power or luxury to act in more ethical ways. As the title of this book says, "Get out of your seat, on your feet and in the streets". It's the "Message of Jesus that is sacred not the method".

The message doesn't change!

8 Jesus, the Anointed One, is always the same—yesterday, today, and forever.

Hebrews 13:8 TPT

The methods can change!

25Jesus, knowing their thoughts, called them to his side and said, "Kings and those with great authority in this world rule oppressively over their subjects, like tyrants. 26But this is not your calling. You will lead by a completely different model.

Matthew 20:25-26 TPT

Whenever you're doing outreaches in your community or city the focus should always be to build relationships and not talking about religion. If you want to have successful outreach ideas, following are a few things you'll need to consider.

WHO ARE YOU TRYING TO REACH?

The members of your community are individuals that have unique interests and personalities. Due to these differences, the same ministry outreach ideas will not have the same impact on everyone. To have an effective outreach event, you need to stay aim focus on the outreach idea. Before you start to plan any outreach idea event, go over the following questions with your staff. What is our organizations niche? When someone tells you to "find your niche, "they are saying that you should find the very specific activity or position that sets you apart and were you can find success or fulfillment. Other questions are, who is your target audience? What your offering, is it something that people need or want? Will your outreach event solve a problem? Have you identified your target audience? This will make your outreach efforts personal and more effective.

You can plan all the outreach ideas you want, but your church or ministry will not see growth unless members of the community and or city attend the outreach events. Once you have your outreach event's specifics planned, you'll also need to plan how you'll market the outreach event. Advertising the event with flyers and signs or sharing it on your church's website or social media accounts will help get the word out and increase the effectiveness of your outreach efforts.

When planning an outreach event, you not only have to take into consideration all the people who will attend, but also all the people that will volunteer to help. It's always wise to think ahead and plan out your outreach ideas. In the last three months (October-December) of the preceding year have a strategy meeting with your creative team for the year ahead. For instance, if you're preparing for next year then the outreach strategies should be completed in the following year, this way all the outreaches are effective and there is a proposed outreach budget.

If church growth is your goal, it's not a good indicator of outreach event success. When planning outreach ideas, set concrete goals that can be measured against, whether that is the number of event attendees, new members acquired, or another metric. These tangible goals will allow you to measure how successful your event was, and these insights will help your church have successful outreach events in the future.

What is an outreach strategy?

An outreach strategy will always help you reach the people in the community that you are targeting. Successful outreach strategies are those that are primarily focused on the people in your community and city.

You can organize a successful outreach event by setting up a food drive, clothing drive or another way of creatively meeting their needs. Whatever outreach event that you plan to set up it is vitally important that you are meeting the needs of the people because "if your ministry is not meeting the needs of the people, then there is no need for your ministry". This will always put you in position to partner with other organizations.

Did you know that there is a very high percentage of people that will attend your church or ministry through an outreach event more than just inviting them to Church? My book titled "Taking it to the Streets" has an extensive chapter on, "How to invite people to Church". As I stated earlier "it's better to build a relationship before you give them religion". Outreach events doesn't need to be expensive to be effective, your team just need to be engaging and be able to connect with people.

It's one thing to invite a friend to church, but it's much easier to invite a friend to a community activity. Also, it's one thing to be invited to church by a friend, but it's much easier to go to church with a friend. Sometimes the latter can help non-believers see that the church is a welcoming place to learn about Christ. Although church outreach might be fun, or take place outside of church property, it should have a mission to share the gospel through action or spoken word. Christ's admonition to serve others and share the gospel is always the driving purpose. Outreach shouldn't be organized haphazardly. It should be a well-thought-out activity with specific objectives in mind. Objectives will differ slightly based on the activity, therefore, documenting these goals are important.

Budgeting

Many church outreach ideas will require a budget. Few ideas will bring back money, so budget accordingly. The good thing about many of the outreach ideas that will be mentioned in the next chapter, is that you can do outreach with minimal cost. Many community outreach activities can be done on church property or in public places such as parks. Don't let a lack of funding discourage your church from doing outreach events.

Location

As mentioned above, your church outreach idea can take place in a variety of places. Whether it's at your church, a park, a community gym, a county fair, or another church, the options are endless. If you plan to do outreach in a public space, make sure you obtain the necessary permits. If there are complaints from the community, you'll have the documentation and approval to continue the activity!

Personnel

All the church outreach ideas in the next chapter will require personnel. Don't be afraid to ask for help and volunteers. You'll be surprised at the skills and abilities of your church members. Accountants, athletes, teachers, nurses, cooks, and farmers can all provide expertise and hard work to make sure the outreach is successful. When in doubt, just ask your congregation for expertise and outreach ideas!

Conclusion

A church, ministry or business should be a major addition in community and city, so it's important for the congregation (Members of the church) to be active beyond Sunday morning services. Remember, "It's not what you do on Sunday morning that invites others to your church, it's what you do through-out the week (Monday-Saturday) that grows the membership of the church. Historically, churches have organized potlucks, provided school and babysitting options, and helped feed the homeless. These days, churches have become much more creative in their outreach. Don't allow the staff and members of the church to turn into monuments, encourage and empower them to have continued movement, how? By "Getting out of your seat, on your feet and in the streets"! Following are almost two hundred outreach ideas to get you started. READY ... SET ...GO!

CHAPTER 6

OUTREACH IDEAS

12 Month Ministry Action Plan (M.A.P.)

1.Adopt-A-Block

As followers of Christ believers are commanded to go house to house

- Simon's House

Jesus used private homes as a base for blessing and a scene for miracles which always led to many healings among the neighbors in the community.

38 Now He arose from the synagogue and entered
Simon's house. But Simon's wife's mother was sick with
a high fever, and they made request of Him concerning
her. 39 So He stood over her and rebuked the fever, and it
left her. And immediately she arose and served them.

Luke 4:38-39 NKJV

-Matthew's House

Jesus always went to secular mainstream occupations to extend a personal invitation for an individual to become a believer in Jesus.

27 After these things He went out and saw a tax collector named Levi, sitting at the tax office. And He said to him, "Follow Me." 28 So he left all, rose up, and followed Him. 29 Then Levi gave Him a great feast in his own house. And there were a great number of tax collectors and others who sat down with them. 30 And their scribes and the Pharisees complained against His disciples, saying, "Why do You eat and drink with tax collectors and sinners?" 31 Jesus answered and said to them, "Those who are well have no need of a physician, but those who are sick. 32 I have not come to call *the* righteous, but sinners, to repentance."

Luke 5:27-32 NKJV

-Pharisee's House

Jesus used a private home of an enemy to witness to another individual

36 Then one of the Pharisees asked Him to eat with him. And He went to the Pharisee's house, and sat down to eat. 37 And behold, a woman in the city who was a sinner, when she knew that *Jesus* sat at the table in the Pharisee's house, brought an alabaster flask of fragrant oil, 38 and stood at His feet behind *Him* weeping; and she began to wash His feet with her tears, and wiped *them*

with the hair of her head; and she kissed His feet and
anointed *them* with the fragrant oil. [39] Now when the
Pharisee who had invited Him saw *this,* he spoke to
himself, saying, "This Man, if He were a prophet, would
know who and what manner of woman *this is* who is
touching Him, for she is a sinner."

Luke 7:36-39 NKJV

[48] Then He said to her, "Your sins are forgiven." [49]
And those who sat at the table with Him began to say to
themselves, "Who is this who even forgives sins?" [50]
Then He said to the woman, "Your faith has saved you.
Go in peace."

Luke 7:48-50 NKJV

-Martha's House

Jesus used Martha's house as a place of word and worship.

[38] Now it happened as they went that He entered a
certain village; and a certain woman named Martha
welcomed Him into her house. [39] And she had a sister
called Mary, who also sat at Jesus' feet and heard His
word. [40] But Martha was distracted with much serving,
and she approached Him and said, "Lord, do You not
care that my sister has left me to serve alone? Therefore
tell her to help me." [41] And Jesus answered and said to
her, "Martha, Martha, you are worried and troubled
about many things. [42] But one thing is needed, and Mary

has chosen that good part, which will not be taken away from her."

Luke 10:38-42 NKJV

-Zacchaeus's House

Jesus went into the home of a rich man who was a Sinner.

9 Then He called His twelve disciples together and gave them power and authority over all demons, and to cure diseases. 2 He sent them to preach the kingdom of God and to heal the sick. 3 And He said to them, "Take nothing for the journey, neither staffs nor bag nor bread nor money; and do not have two tunics apiece. 4 "Whatever house you enter, stay there, and from there depart. 5 And whoever will not receive you, when you go out of that city, shake off the very dust from your feet as a testimony against them." 6 So they departed and went through the towns, preaching the gospel and healing everywhere. 7 Now Herod the tetrarch heard of all that was done by Him; and he was perplexed, because it was said by some that John had risen from the dead, 8 and by some that Elijah had appeared, and by others that one of the old prophets had risen again. 9 Herod said, "John I have beheaded, but who is this of whom I hear such things?" So he sought to see Him. 10 And the apostles, when they had returned, told Him all that they had done. Then He took them and went aside privately into a deserted place belonging to the city called Bethsaida.

Luke 19:1-10 NKJV

-People at their place of business

Jesus entered homes and places of business to teach, preach, heal and to forgive sins and make disciples.

5 So it was, as the multitude pressed about Him to
hear the word of God, that He stood by the Lake of
Gennesaret, 2 and saw two boats standing by the lake;
but the fishermen had gone from them and were
washing *their* nets. 3 Then He got into one of the boats,
which was Simon's, and asked him to put out a little from
the land. And He sat down and taught the multitudes
from the boat. 4 When He had stopped speaking, He said
to Simon, "Launch out into the deep and let down your
nets for a catch."

5 But Simon answered and said to Him, "Master, we
have toiled all night and caught nothing; nevertheless at
Your word I will let down the net." 6 And when they had
done this, they caught a great number of fish, and their
net was breaking. 7 So they signaled to *their* partners in
the other boat to come and help them. And they came
and filled both the boats, so that they began to sink. 8
When Simon Peter saw *it,* he fell down at Jesus' knees,
saying, "Depart from me, for I am a sinful man, O Lord!"

9 For he and all who were with him were astonished
at the catch of fish which they had taken; 10 and so also
were James and John, the sons of Zebedee, who were
partners with Simon. And Jesus said to Simon, "Do not be
afraid. From now on you will catch men." 11 So when they

had brought their boats to land, they forsook all and followed Him.

Luke 5:1-11 NKJV

-The first disciples were won in a spiritual conversation in the home of Jesus

Philip and Nathaniel

35 Again, the next day, John stood with two of his disciples. 36 And looking at Jesus as He walked, he said, "Behold the Lamb of God!" 37 The two disciples heard him speak, and they followed Jesus. 38 Then Jesus turned, and seeing them following, said to them, "What do you seek?" They said to Him, "Rabbi" (which is to say, when translated, Teacher), "where are You staying?" 39 He said to them, "Come and see." They came and saw where He was staying, and remained with Him that day (now it was about the tenth hour).

John 1:35-39 NKJV

43 The following day Jesus wanted to go to Galilee, and He found Philip and said to him, "Follow Me." 44 Now Philip was from Bethsaida, the city of Andrew and Peter. 45 Philip found Nathanael and said to him, "We have found Him of whom Moses in the law, and also the prophets, wrote—Jesus of Nazareth, the son of Joseph." 46 And Nathanael said to him, "Can anything good come out of Nazareth?" Philip said to him, "Come and see." 47 Jesus saw Nathanael coming toward Him, and said of him, "Behold, an Israelite indeed, in whom is no deceit!"

48 Nathanael said to Him, “How do You know me?” Jesus answered and said to him, “Before Philip called you, when you were under the fig tree, I saw you.”

John 1:43-48 NKJV

Nicodemus

3 There was a man of the Pharisees named Nicodemus, a ruler of the Jews. 2 This man came to Jesus by night and said to Him, “Rabbi, we know that You are a teacher come from God; for no one can do these signs that You do unless God is with him.” 3 Jesus answered and said to him, “Most assuredly, I say to you, unless one is born again, he cannot see the kingdom of God.” 4 Nicodemus said to Him, “How can a man be born when he is old? Can he enter a second time into his mother’s womb and be born?” 5 Jesus answered, “Most assuredly, I say to you, unless one is born of water and the Spirit, he cannot enter the kingdom of God. 6 That which is born of the flesh is flesh, and that which is born of the Spirit is spirit. 7 Do not marvel that I said to you, ‘You must be born again.’

John 3:1-7 NKJV

-Jesus preached on house tops

27 “Whatever I tell you in the dark, speak in the light; and what you hear in the ear, preach on the housetops.

Matthew 10:27 NKJV

Adopt-A-Block can be done every day of the week, but it's wise to only start out with what you can be consistent with. The following are basic Saturday morning steps to prepare for Adopt-a-Block outreach.

1. Meet at Adopt-a-Block headquarters at 9:30 am

2. Pray from 9:30 to 9:45 am for divine appointments

3 Load vehicles with equipment at 9:45 to 10:15 am

4 Leave at 10:15 am for Adopt-a-Block sites

5. Return to Adopt-a-Block headquarters at 1:00 pm

The Adopt-a-Block team is organized within the church. Members of the congregation form teams of five people. Each team has a site leader, co-leader, and three section leaders. A section of the community is mapped out and streets are designated for house to house or door to door evangelism "witnessing". A packet of materials is given to each site leader that includes the location of the Adopt-a-Block area, tracts, church schedule, follow up forms, Bible, pencils, etc., one member of the team should carry a Bible. Personal belongings should be left at the Adopt-a-Block headquarters.

Before going to the Adopt-a-Block block sites, teams are prayed over and sent out for approximately two hours. There is usually one team assigned per street "a team on each side of the street". The teams remain within sight of each other. As the teams go from door to door everyone is offered the prayer of salvation and immediately after is given a track, a schedule of church services along with a personal invitation to the weekend service. The team will gather the individuals (If married gather the spouse and children name), address, phone number, birthdays, and anniversary dates. The purpose for the contact information is so there can be a successful follow up. As I travel through-out the United States teaching in evangelism and outreach intensives I often remind churches leaders, "When you don't follow-up they will fall through". The data information that was collected from individuals are given to the Adopt-a-Block site Co-leader when the teams return to the Adopt-a-Block Headquarters.

STEP 1 – PICK A CENTRAL LOCATION

Before starting your Adopt-a-Block outreach you first must pray about a central location as a base for your service to the community. The central location will be where your volunteers will consistently serve and meet the needs of the neighborhood on a weekly basis.

When choosing the central location, find an area that is easily accessible for those in the community but not in a location that will be a difficult to gather everyone, such as blocking the sidewalk or stopping traffic. If possible, find a grassy area because they are great for activities for children. Make sure it's a safe area so that there will not be any injury to children or adults. Always leave the central location cleaner than what it was before you started.

The central location will serve as an advertisement for the Adopt-a-Block outreach site. Everyone in the community may not be aware of the activities provided by Adopt-a-Block, but families will be drawn to the central location when they see what programs are available for the community. As I stated before "If you're ministry is not meeting the needs of the community, then there is no need for your ministry in the community"

STEP 2- SURVEY A FOUR BLOCK RADIUS OF THE CENTRAL LOCATION

To know the specific needs of the community, the first thing you should do is a survey of a three-block radius surrounding your central location. While canvassing the area, promote where the central location activities will be taking place. The second thing is to gather suggestions from individuals and families through-out the community by creating a survey with the name, address, phone number, and email address. Following are questions to help you create an informative survey.

FIVE QUESTION SURVEY

What would you like to see happen in your neighborhood?

How can we assist you to make the community a better place to live?

What is the biggest need in your community?

Since you've lived in this community what is the biggest improvement you've seen?

What has most negatively affected your neighborhood since you've lived here?

After surveying the area, you will see specific ideas mentioned by those in the community. The areas of need repeated on the survey, such as programs for children, are a great starting point for Adopt-A-Block in the community. When you take notes of what the residents would like to see happen, how they can be assisted, and what's their biggest need is, you now have created a follow-up list to invite those in the community to be a part of the upcoming Adopt-A-Block launch!

STEP 3 – LAUNCH ADOPT-A-BLOCK AT CENTRAL LOCATION

The goal of Adopt-A-Block is to build relationships and the key to its success is consistency. When Adopt-A-Block launches at a specific location, it is a promise to the community that, rain, or shine, that your team will be there to serve consistently. Your commitment to the community will speak louder than your activities for the community. Don't be disappointed if the first Adopt-a-Block Day number of people is low. For more than thirty-two years I've never allowed the number of people, that attended an outreach event discourage me. Remember, the individuals who show up are the ones who are called to be there. "Don't count the numbers but make the numbers count" in other words, serve the individuals that have showed up. There have been numerous times that I have spoken in churches and the Pastor said to me, "We can't do an Adopt-a-Block outreach because we only have a few people in our church. My response to Him or Her is always the same, "Jesus changed the whole world with twelve and less, what's your problem. I continue to always say that "If you try to reach a thousand people you might not touch one person, but if you touch one person you will always reach a thousand people".

Once the surveys are completed, you're now ready to promote the Adopt-a-Block launch by walking through-out the community, over the telephone, email, and/or text. Furthermore, you will now have specific areas of needs identified by those in the community, by "Finding a need and fill it and a hurting hurt and heal it". Meeting the immediate needs of the community is the fastest way to build relationships. Immediate needs may include but are not limited to food and clothing giveaways, activities for children, and picking up trash just name a few. As you continue to read this list of outreach ideas, you will be empowered to do many more outreaches. Following is the "E" of Adopt-a-Block outreach.

When an individual or family shows up to their first community Adopt-a-Block outreach event its usually an "Emergency" (Emergency is a serious unexpected situation requiring immediate action).

When the same individuals show up a second time they are "Expecting" (Expecting means to regard something as likely to happen) to receive what they were giving the first time.

When the same individuals show up a third time, they're starting to feel a sense of community "Entitlement" (Entitlement is the fact of having a right to something) and are excited about the outreach events that are taking place within their community.

As individuals are consistently showing up to the Adopt-a-Block central location, this is a great time to start "Empowering" (Empowering is the action of giving someone the authority or means to do something) them with the Gospel to go make disciples.

The Adopt-A-Block leadership, characteristics, and responsibilities are as follows.

A great Adopt-a-Block team possess an "EFP" character. Which means that they are.

Effective – To be Effective is to be successful in producing a desire or intended result.

Friendly – To be friendly to someone or something exhibiting the characteristics of a friend, such as being kind, helpful or affectionate.

Passionate – To be passionate about something is to have a very strong feeling about something or a strong belief in something,

A great Adopt-a-Block team are "FAT" in their responsibilities. Which means that they are.

Faithful – To be faithful is to remain loyal and steadfast to what you have been called to do.

Available – To be available is to be ready and use for the assignment that has been giving to you to do.

Teachable – Willing to learn and capable of learning.

THE DIRECTOR

The director is the "Visionary" for the overall structure and implementation for the Adopt-a-Block program.

SITE LEADERS

The site leaders are "Passionate" about the Adopt-a-Block site and their responsibility is to provide the vision to make events happen. Also, Adopt-a-Block site leaders' responsibility is to oversee all site operations and develop new site leaders.

CO-LEADERS

The co-leaders are the "Administrators" their assignment is to support the Adopt-a-Block site leaders' vision to make sure that all the outreach events are legal, have funding, and are being promoted.

Section leader number one is "Energetic"

Section leader number two is "Outgoing"

Section leader number three is "Friendly"

Section leaders are supportive and take the initiative every week, in building relationships with the individuals and families that attend the Adopt-a-Block central location, door to door, working the food and clothing giveaways and leading the children's activities. They are "energetic", "outgoing" and "friendly".

The Adopt-a-Block director should be in contact with the site leader to cast vision and direction for the program. The Adopt-a-Block site leader responsibility is to communicate all request from the Co-leaders to the director. Also, the site leader is responsible for passing the information from the director to the Co-leaders and section leaders. Constant communication will ensure that all needs of the Adopt-a-Block sites are being met. One way to facilitate regular communication is to have a weekly creative Adopt-a-Block team and to create a weekly report. The weekly report should consist of the following log sheets from the sites; Adopt-a-Block needs list and Adopt-a-Block prayer request. Also, for all Adopt-a-Block volunteers you will need to create the following three forms for signatures: Minor's Information & Outreach Release Form, Adult Information & Outreach Release Form, and a Release of Liability Agreement.

2.Apartment Complex

Apartment complexes are great areas to market because you get an opportunity to engage with people who are in transition, such as individuals who have moved from other cities with new jobs or people that are starting over in life. People that live in apartment complexes are often forgot about, but it is the most populated area of people in one spot even if it is temporary. Most people that live in apartment complexes are there for at least five years because they're looking to buy a house or improve their lifestyle. To start a successful apartment complex outreach you first need to contact and build a relationship with the property manager or agency to get permission to place your advertisement into their welcome package and once a relationship is built then the office manager can place your brochure (A brochure is a flyer that is used to pass information about something or it's an informative paper document that can be folded into a template, pamphlet, or leaflet) inside their welcome package. What are welcome packages? Welcome packages are given to potential new residents of the apartment. Included inside the welcome package are brochures of different restaurants, shopping centers, furniture stores etc., so placing your church, ministry, or business advertisement in a brochure can bring exposure to your organization, to individuals or families that are in transition. Remember, that your brochures must be approved by the agency and or management office. Most apartment managers do not want churches, ministry or businesses passing out brochures on private property to their residents, putting them on cars or putting door hangers on resident doors without their consent. Always work with in the apartment complex guidelines and "do the right thing, because it's the right thing to do".

3.After School Tutoring

An after-school tutoring programs will require financial, spiritual, and volunteer support. It's important that all qualified individuals must participate into the program for it to be successful. When your church or ministry starts doing after school program and is committed to serving children, the church will always be relevant in the community. For the program to be successful the pastor of the church must support the after-school tutoring program. Meet with your creative team to determine the focus of the program. Consideration should be given to educational goals, spiritual goals, nutritional goals, and physical fitness goals. All are significant components of most after school tutoring programs. Following are a few Questions to ask yourself before getting started. What is the population of children that the program will target? How many children can the program effectively support? What type of insurance will the after-school tutoring program needs to cover incidents and accidents during the duration of the program?

Write down the vision statement, mission statement and program goals. Once you get the Pastors approval put the vision, mission, and program goals on official letterhead to present to potential volunteer or paid staff workers. Create program rules and regulations for the after-school tutoring program students and qualified paid and volunteer workers.

Advertise within the church community the need for volunteer or paid workers. Submit an official background check for each paid and volunteer worker. Select the after-school tutoring staff who will work with the after-school program. Provide the staff with the official vision, mission statements and program goals. Advertise the after-school tutoring program enrollment to the target audience through word of mouth, church announcements, radio, and the newspaper. Determine enrollment cut-off date and establish a day to meet with the program participants' parents and guardians to review policies, rules, and regulations.

4.Art Show

Most communities and cities have several artists, and chances are that they don't think of the church as a big supporter of the arts. You can change that! Invite local artist to do showings of their local artwork in your church. You can also feature local artists at bigger events throughout the year. This can provide a connection to your community and city.

5.Baby Sitting

Do you have young couples in your congregation? Want to provide a free service for your community? Free babysitting for date night could be a good way to appreciate young families in your area. Promote a monthly free babysitting event at your church. Parents at your church and from the community will drop off their children for a few hours and enjoy some quiet time. Babysitting is expensive so parents will love this! Just make sure you have experienced volunteers to take care of all the children.

6.Books to distribute throughout your community, city, state, and the world

Writing your own book or manual is another great outreach marketing tool to use when trying to get your message heard by millions of people. Get your plans, visions and dreams that are in your head and heart onto paper. To start creating your book, just do the following three things.

7. Write it
8. Type it
9. Upload your manuscripts to the publisher's website

If you don't feel like you have the writing skills, but you like to talk, you can create an audio book. If you don't want to be responsible for handling paper or hardback books you can create an eBook or why not create all three it doesn't matter how you do it just do something.

7.Bus Outreach

Many churches, ministries and businesses are not experiencing growth in their organization. The bus outreach is one of the most important ministries that can be used as a great marketing outreach, for serving low-income individuals and families through-out the community that lacks transportation. If your church, ministry, or business cannot afford a bus or worried about insurance or expenses for maintenance on a bus, you can always rent a bus with a driver and never worry about anything. Call your local charter service or school district to get more information.

8.Big Days

Big days are known as the following Easter, Mother's Day, Father's Day, Thanksgiving and Christmas. On these five days make sure that you keep everything relevant. Following these outreach ideas, I have compiled a twelve-month Ministry Action Plan (M.A.P.) that will give you a yearly guide for other big day outreach ideas.

9.Business Cards

Business cards is one of the most important parts of your brand identity. It's a common misconception that in the age of smartphones and social media, that business cards are no longer important. Don't believe it! When you meet someone face to face, your business card Is the key to leaving a lasting and positive impression. Your business card is a relatively small investment that can scale relationships, sales, and profits! Through experience, I've learned several ways to maximize how business cards can have a huge impact, and I hope you'll find them helpful.

SEVEN WAYS TO USE YOUR BUSINESS CARD EFFECTIVELY

1. Invest in Quality cards.

When you meet someone, your business card continues to represent you long after you depart. A thin card that easily bends, creases, or gets dog ears gives acceptable impression that you're not at the top of your game. Make a strong, lasting impression by using strong card stock and quality printing. It'll cost a little bit more, but it's worth it!

2. Make a card that fits your brand.

Your card should be true to your brand identity and appropriate for your field. Style your card to project the image that you want to portray. If you're an attorney serving corporate clients, then a colorful, glossy card is probably not a good choice, an extreme example but you get the idea. On the other hand, if you work in a creative field, you can probably be colorful on your cards. Whatever you choose to do, just make sure it represents you, your company, and the image you want to convey.

3. Hire a designer.

Most printers have business card templates from which you can choose. These work well for the basic layout, but don't offer many varieties if you want to get a little creative. If you're not a designer yourself, it might not be a good idea to try to create a look yourself. For a layout and design that stands out, using a professional designer can really set your card apart. This doesn't have to cost a lot, you can hire a designer online Ray Hampton Outreach Ministries have used multiple online services.

4. Drive traffic to your website.

Your card should always contain the basics, which is your name, title, company name, address, phone number, e-mail, and website. You can use your card to inspire people to visit your website. Give them a compelling reason to pull it up. If you have a free offer on your website, why not feature it on your card? Include a call to action and let them know why they need to be on your website now! In addition to showing your web address on your card you can add a QR code, that way all they need to do is scan your card with their smartphone and they're taking straight to your website. As you continue to read through the outreach ideas, there is a section on what is a QR code and the importance of having a QR code.

5. Create different cards for different audiences.

Many entrepreneurs provide different products and services two diverse customer Groups. Maybe you have one set of services for consumers, and another for business clients. You can create tailor made business cards specifically for your target audience. This way you can address their specific needs rather than trying to have a catch all card. I have several business cards I can choose from depending on the situation, such as speaking engagements, outreach, church, and business.

6. Shop around for a great print shop.

If you live in a metropolitan area, there are probably many print shops to choose from. If you don't, that's not a problem, you can find a lot of good print shops online. Look for a printer that has testimonials of satisfied customers and examples of their work. Also, make sure their prices are competitive, but be aware that the shop that's the lowest bid might not provide the level of service you're looking for. Ray Hampton Outreach Ministries has local printers and online shops that we use depending on the need. We've developed strong relationships with printers over the years, and it's great to know that we can rely on them to turn around a job on a short notice with excellent quality and first-class service.

7. Always have your cards on hand.

There's nothing worse than making an important connection and not having your business card with you. Safeguard against this by always keeping your cards wherever you go. Invest in several business card holders so they stay pristine. To keep cards pristine means to keep your business cards looking in its original condition, which is clean, fresh, and looking brand new. Keep cards in your purse, briefcase, your car's glove compartment, at your office and at home. Make it a habit to always take your business cards wherever you go.

Look at your business card. Does it convey who you are, and what your brand is all about? Is it high quality? Is it professionally designed and visually appealing? Does it Give a compelling reason for others to get connected with you when they visit your website? If not, consider upgrading your cards, it could increase the quality of your connections which will increase your profits. Get ready to receive "profits from your passion"! Think of all the places you can hand out or leave your business card. Make it a habit to get your card in the hands of potential customers, client, or business partners every day this week. Start giving out your business cards today as if big things are on the way, because they are! Go somewhere you've never been and meet new people. You must "change your comfort zone to change your money zone"! You will start seeing results quickly.

10.Branding

Branding is your identity and will place you on a map to show others not just who you are but what you're all about. Branding also identifies you and put your face on a product. When you are scaling your brand, it is very important to know who you are trying to reach. For example, if you are trying to let everyone know that you're a family church or business don't just put the picture of the pastor or owner on the photo it is very important that you put a picture of families. If you want to attract singles then you should brand singles in your advertisement, if you want to attract a multicultural congregation then put different nationalities in your advertisement. Too many times I have seen pastors and business owners, non-profit and profit organizations who want to attract a mix of all races of people, but they're only branding one race. People will not hear what you say all the time, but they will respond to what you advertise. Whatever age you are trying to attract it is very important that you advertise that age. If you would like your church, ministry, or business branding to effectively work everyone from the pastor to the one sitting in the pews, from the business owner to every staff employee volunteer or paid must be on one accord. Other important branding things to remember is that your color scheme within your organization structure and font style in your writing of literature and signage must be consistent. Getting professional pictures taken is also about branding because your image is everything the way you dress, talk, and carry yourself, will also determine what kind of people you will attract. Professional photographers can apply makeup to your face that covers skin and blemishes to bring out your natural beauty. Remember, whether you choose an image or not you have already chosen your image. People will brand you for what you do or not do!

11.Billboards

Billboards are great advertisement, find a heavy traffic area that you would like to saturate, now you have just taken your first step toward community and citywide outreach marketing. The second step is to notice that on each billboard sign there's a number on it which will help you with your conversation when calling the agency. Once you call the agency give them the numbers that was on the sign and location. Now you're ready for outreach marketing, the people in the city are now looking for you instead of you looking for them. The question you might still be wondering is, why should I use billboards for advertising for my church, ministry, or business? The answer is simple because everyone sees it!

12.Bus stops

Bus stops are a great way of outreaching to the entire community that are already traveling throughout the city. As they are waiting for their bus to arrive they're also looking at your advertisement that has been posted which means that your church, ministry or business is consistently on their mind throughout the day, just think about the thousands of people that are riding on the city transit or metro buses with your name implanted in their mind all day and if only one percent showed up at your church, ministry or business it's worth the outreach marketing.

13.Block Party

If your church has a large available outside space, or even a good-sized parking lot, you can put on an incredible block party. Make sure there are plenty of games, food, and entertainment, and you've just started a created a way to connect with the community. You'll will need to invest in some flyers or invitations, go door to door around the neighborhood. If your church isn't the best location, find a couple of different families in the church and host block parties from their homes.

14.Backpack and school supplies drive

Determine Your Goal

After deciding you want to start a backpack and school supplies give away, you need to determine your goal and create a plan. Tailor your drive to a specific item. If you prefer to generally ask for all manner of school supplies, that works too. Either way, planning helps you communicate your mission to others and go forward. Another tip for starting a back pack and school-supply drive for your community is to make the drive excited to be part of. Understand that you cannot do this alone you need your friends, local businesses, and other passionate people or organizations to make your drive run smoothly. Local businesses in particular want to communicate an investment in the community to build consumer trust, so be sure to talk through a partnership with as many businesses as you can. Also know that assessing others' interest is when you secure volunteers to help you acquire, store, and deliver your back packs and school supplies. This too you cannot do alone.

Determine a School's Need

Next, ask people who know their school district what they think students need. Teachers in your area are excellent resources because they can tell you their needs and their students' needs as you ask for ideas for the drive. If you want a more holistic idea of schools' needs, begin communicating with administration officials. They can not only give you an idea of what students need district-wide but connect you with people and resources to make your backpack and school supplies drive a success.

Give Potential Participants Options

As you shift to planning the drive itself, consider giving people different ways they can give. Some people are used to and prefer giving concrete items, while others appreciate the ease of giving money to your cause. Set up a simple way for people to give money if they so choose. You can even set up an online channel for donations if you have the technical capability.

Spread the Word

Once you have determined what your school-supply drive will raise and who will make it happen, you can begin marketing your drive. You can spread the word through social media and through the school's own network.

Through social media

Social media is a powerful tool for networking. If you're the parent of a current or recent student at the school you're giving to, check to see if there are online communities for that school or your city. You may already be in one perfect for your marketing purposes. If you aren't a parent, search for one of these social media groups to share your idea. You may even get more help putting on the drive by doing this.

Through the School

Make use of the school's network. If you gain their support, they can notify the public in their own way. Perhaps through them, you can take advantage of the city's communication channels to help create open doors.

Hold Your Supply Drive

Now it's time for the backpack and school supply drive. This can be a one-day event, weekend event, or even several weeks. The benefit to a quick drive is you don't have to wait for supplies and can build up public awareness for that certain day, weekend, or weeks. Meanwhile, the benefit to holding a longer drive is you may raise more from people unable or unwilling to attend an event.

A Weeks-Long Drive

You can be more flexible with a longer school-supplies drive. Installing drop-off containers that volunteers routinely check allows for easy, contactless donations. Throughout the weeks, it would help notify people of the drive's progress and recommunicate how they can still help you reach your goal.

Deliver the Supplies You Receive

Finally, when you have your school supplies in hand, you need to deliver everything to the school or organization you're partnering with. Make sure you have enough volunteers on hand to help. Talk with school administrators about delivering the donations. *Go to YouTube and search for 2010 Backpack Giveaway* to check the Ray Hampton Outreach Ministries Backpack and School Supplies give away.

15.Back to School Party

The fall is upon us, which means it's back to school for many families. This time of the year is full of excitement, but it also presents a variety of challenges for parents and children alike. As the church, this is an excellent time of the year to meet the practical needs of your community, which will provide you with many opportunities to present the gospel. Following are four back-to-school outreach ideas for you to consider.

1. Purchase school supplies and clothes

Back-to-school equals a lot of expenses for families. They need to buy school supplies, clothes, backpacks, and possibly arrange for childcare. However, many of these families don't have the disposable income to spare. The needs of families will vary from church to church but make plans on meeting these needs to the best of your ability.

2. Back-to-school event

Putting together a back-to-school event will help you to gather families together and connect with them in a lighthearted environment. Depending on your community, you may have many new families who have moved to the area. So, back-to-school events can also help these new families meet people in the community.

3. Serve teachers

Serving as a teacher is a wonderful calling that requires a significant sacrifice. Their days are long, and the challenges to graciously tend to the children they teach can be taxing.

From providing teachers with gift cards or coffee to organizing a teacher-appreciation event during or after school hours, can go a long way in expressing your appreciation of their work for the families in your community.

4. Adopt a school

What schools are in your community? Commit to regularly praying for these schools, open your facilities for them to use, and organize teacher appreciation events. There are several more things you can consider, but prayerfully think about what the schools in your community need and do what you can do to meet their needs.

16.Back-to-School Fair

Help parents and children in your community celebrate the new school year by hosting a fun event at your church. Set up stations around your church parking lot or campus—face painting, photo booth, ring toss, cupcake walk, craft table. Invite the teachers, coaches, and principals from local schools to be your celebrity guests. Serve hot dogs and cotton candy to give it a real carnival feel.

17.Bible Study

Offer a secure and non-threatening opportunity for people to study God's Word and build authentic relationships. The key, however, is creating quality, intentional Bible study group experiences that grow out of a clear commitment to make them work. Pray about whether to start a small group and that God will prepare you for the next few steps in this journey. Without a doubt, this is the most neglected step. But this is a very important one because small group ministry requires leaders who have a heart for people and are willing to invest themselves in the lives of group members. Developing a mission based on prayer and commitment will help you set the course. A vision helps focus your efforts in one direction rather than chasing off in multiple directions. It's good to know who you want to reach through your group. Most of the time, you can figure this out just by looking around your community and asking a few questions:

- Who is accessible to you?
- Who do you already know?

- Do you want to offer an early morning Bible study for business leaders?
- Are there young moms in your community who need a support system?
- Could you organize a prayer and Bible study group where young adults hang out?

Think about the people around your church. How many have been there for years? Most likely, someone has tried this before. Some have failed and some have succeeded. Bring together those people and other leaders who can offer fresh ideas and wisdom for creating something new. How frequent will your group meet and what types of studies will you have? One way to choose your approach is to start with a calendar. Plan from a yearly perspective, if possible, then focus in on each month. This is a great time to dream about what God can do in your community. Be mindful of your group members and what their needs are while you plan. Don't forget to allow for some flexibility in your planning.

Again, the nature of small group studies is different from an ongoing Sunday School class. Identify potential leaders and their strengths, equip them based on the unique needs of the small group target and commission them to fulfill the tasks for which they have been trained.

The small group approach needs one central leader who coordinates the work. This leader can evaluate the effectiveness of current studies. He or she will also identify other needs to address and plan for groups.

Start every group with a leader and an apprentice. Every leader should be training an apprentice to someday lead his or her own group. Equip them to invest themselves in others as their leaders have in them. Complete different studies or books, evaluate and plan new groups based on your experience. Never be afraid to adapt. Use all the organizational tools you can find to create a life-changing small group ministry.

18. Baby supplies for the Homeless

Yes, it's sad, but there are many homeless people who have babies. Think about the most expensive things mothers need for the baby: diapers, baby wipes, or clothes. The big items mentioned can be difficult for a mother with a home above her head to buy now. Imagine one without a home.

19.Blankets Give Away to the Homeless

Homelessness is a growing problem in America, millions of people live on the streets or in shelters. The problem has been getting worse, due to a combination of factors such as the cost of living, wages, and affordable housing. While there are many causes of homelessness, one of the most visible is the lack of blankets for homeless people during cold weather. Every winter, dozens of homeless people die from exposure to the elements. While some shelters do provide blankets, they are often in short supply and cannot meet the demand. As a result, many homeless people are forced to sleep without blankets, putting themselves at risk of hypothermia and frostbite.

Blankets can provide warmth and comfort to those who are struggling, and they are one of the most needed items at homeless shelters. For many of us, blankets are a source of comfort and warmth on cold nights. But for the homeless, blankets can mean so much more. A blanket can provide a barrier against the cold, both physically and emotionally. It can be a reminder that someone cares, that there are people who are willing to help. That's why blankets are one of the most needed items. Blankets not only provide warmth, but also a sense of security and safety.

What type of blankets are best for the homeless?

There are a few things to keep in mind. First, you'll want something that is durable and will stand up to repeated washings. Blankets for homeless people tend to get a lot of wear and tear, so it's important to choose something that will last. Additionally, you'll want to choose blankets that are warm and comfortable. Homeless people often have to sleep outdoors, so it's important to choose blankets that will keep them warm, such as a thermal blanket. Finally, you'll want to choose blankets that are easy to clean. Many homeless people don't have access to laundry facilities, so it's important to choose blankets that can be easily cleaned by hand.

20. Bedding items for the Homeless

Sometimes homeless people go to shelters for a warm place to sleep, and there's a serious demand for more bedding materials. You can always contact your local shelter to see if they need bedding items, and even if you don't want to donate to shelters, you can always give bedding materials to homeless people who sleep by the roadside or under the bridge. Trust me, they really would appreciate it!

21.Book Club

Books clubs are a way to bring like-minded people together. Most people either love reading or dislike it. For those that love it, give them a place to meet and discuss popular books. The book club might have a theme, or it could jump from one genre to the next. It could also have a faith-based approach in sharing the gospel in a non-threatening atmosphere.

22.Backpacking Trip

A backpacking trip can bring us closer to nature and allows us to spend time in God's perfect creation. Backpacking trips aren't usually for large groups, but a church could use the activity to connect with people in their community. With no distractions, time spent around an evening campfire promotes conversation and it's an opportunity to share one's faith with others.

23.Connect Cards

Connect cards is another great tool for your members/customers to invite people to their church, ministry, or business. Connect cards are great because it allows the inviter to have a personal card to give to the invitee. When the invitee shows up to the church/business the inviter name will be signed on the back of the card, which allows the greeter ministry to know who invited the invitee. All it takes is a business size card with your service/operating time and location on it. On the back of the card there will be a place where the inviter will sign their name.

24.Conference call

Instead of one-on-one calling, call waiting or three-way calling how about using your same phone to talk to over one hundred to thousand people at one time and be able to have the capability of engaging in a conversation not just with one individual but to multiple individuals. You can be the teacher and your participants will be the student. Each participant can respond to your questions, where everyone can hear. At the end of the lesson, you can open the conversation up for individual questions by explaining to your students, members, partners, congregation, or business associates with numbered demands that they will be able to push on their phone. You can also record the conversation/lesson so anyone can come back as many times as they want to listen to what had been communicated. I remember one winter season in Seattle, Washington we received a lot of snow, and no one was able to make it to the building to attend the church service. Instead, we had online church service by using call service to call every member at one time, email service to email every member and a texting service to text every member to let them know to call in to a conference call number at certain time that will connect us all together. After the conversation was over all members of the church were directed to the church website to give their financial contribution through online giving to whatever outreach event that we were doing at the time. You can even have the capability of sending the recorded meeting by email, to anyone you would like just by downloading it onto your computer. This is a free service and all you need to do is go online to freeconferencing.com to start growing your church, ministry or Business Today. The following six steps will introduce you to a new way of conducting your meetings by doing online meetings in time of emergency or non-emergency.

1.Go to freeconferencing.com

2.You will be giving a call-in number

3.A back up number

4.A recorded message number

5.A host participant code

6.A participant code

25.Counseling Center

Developing a Church Counseling Center

1. Know your congregation and its needs

2. Know your community and its needs

3. Be willing to start small

4. Form a committee that will brainstorm new ministry ideas and will also be willing to divide up the work.

5. Find effective speakers by listening to what other churches do

26.Chaplincy

Duties and Responsibilities

A chaplain's most important job is to provide religious services, spiritual guidance, and counseling to those in need. A chaplain gives sermons to encourage spirituality and provide comfort. A chaplain who works in a hospital or hospice facility provides counseling and spiritual guidance for patients, their families, and even the hospital staff. Chaplains may also provide educational programs or conversion counseling to youth or prisoners. Chaplains can perform religious rites such as weddings and funerals as well. Depending on their work environment, chaplains may plan and coordinate retreats and training for others who perform religious services and spiritual counseling.

27.Church musical

Have you ever thought about hosting a city-wide church musical at your church? Call every church through-out the city and invite their Choir or soloist to represent their church for a night of praise and worship filled with fun, food, and fellowship. Allow each church to sing two songs. You can even have drawings for giveaways such as gift certificates to sporting events or dinner for two, for the people that are in attendance. Church musicals are a great way to build unity in your community!

28.Community or City Ice Cream social

The main goal of an ice cream social is to gather around some friends and relatives for a casual party where everyone has fun. An ice cream social is perfect for a spring or summer outreach where you can invite the whole community. It can be outside, and you can offer a wide range of homemade ice creams, toppings, sauces, and anything else you want. Besides, since everyone loves ice cream, this is a perfect opportunity to gather both adults and children. You can even play some games which allows you to engage with your guests so you can build long lasting relationships.

THE WORLDS BIGGEST BANNA SPLIT

Go purchase a brand-new six-foot gutter or longer (The type that are used on homes). Clean it out, get multiple giant tubs of vanilla, strawberry, and chocolate ice cream. Buy multiple toppings like chocolate, strawberry and caramel syrup, large containers of sprinkles and peanuts, a box of bananas, a big jar of cherries, a huge container of whipped cream topping and thousand cones and bowls.

29.Community or City Barbeque

A church barbeque may seem like a private event, but it doesn't have to be. It's the perfect time to invite friends to a low-pressure social activity where people can be outside, enjoying great weather, conversation, and food. It's perfect for families with children. Children can interact with other children and make new friends. Organizing a BBQ competition is a perfect way to bring a community together and feed people. Provide a cash prize for the winner and grow this event each summer!

30.Community or City Harvest Party

Lots of families are looking for safe, fun things to do in October. This is a wonderful way for your church or ministry to reach not just the community but the whole city. You can host a harvest party and provide games, snacks, and candy. This can provide you with an opportunity to get to know parents and their children. You can also invite the city to the "Trunk or Treat" where people from the church gather in the parking lot, fill their decorated trunks with candy, and allow children to go from trunk (Car) to trunk (Car) as they fill their bags and buckets with lots of candy. Trunk and Treats are generally well attended, but it can be kind of chaotic and hard to make genuine connections with visitors, so have your outreach team ready to engage with the people.

31.Community or City Job Fair

Have you ever thought about hosting a Job fair at the church? In case you might be wondering what a job fair is, it is an event where employers and job seekers meet to discuss employment opportunities. Job fairs can be a great way for employers to find talented employees and for job seekers to learn about new vacancies. Job fairs allow both employers and job seekers to network with each other and establish potential connections.

There are certainly some rights and wrongs you should keep in mind. A good job fair should create excitement in the community and people should arrive with a WOW attitude of what they are getting ready to experience and give them plenty to think about when they leave! It is also important to know that job fairs are not the same as networking events. Job fairs are designed to find candidates who fit a company's needs while networking events should be more personal. They are also a great networking opportunity for both groups once you know how to plan one. I often say through-out my travels the following phrase "If you're not networking, you're not-working"

32.Community or City festival

Go build relationships with local vendors from all around the city and invite them to set up booths at the church to sell their products and services. Also make sure there are food booths and games for the children. Don't do it as a one-time event, be consistent and eventually your church will establish itself as an important part of the community.

33.Christmas wrapping booth

A great outreach that your church youth group, women's, missions, or outreach ministry can do during the holidays is a wrapping booth. Go to the local city mall an offer a free or donation accepted gift wrapping booth. As the gifts are being wrap this is also great way to engage with thousands of individuals that you normally wouldn't had met.

34.Cold bottle of water (on hot days)

Buy some cases of water and keep them in your car. When you see someone on the streets hand them a bottle of water. Dehydration is a major threat to many on the streets and this water is lifesaving to those who can't find any. You might even want to consider getting some frozen bottled water and drive around to give them out. Get creative and have your church, ministry or business label wrapped on the bottle with your contact information. You can even use a verse that says, "I was thirsty, and you gave me something to drink".

WOW! This is one of the most amazing simplest outreach events that your church, ministry or business can do. Can you imagine on a hot sunny day, especially when it's over 90 degrees and people are walking down the street with sweat coming down their forehead or drivers with no air condition and see a sign saying, "free cold-water bottles". I guarantee you someone will stop to receive one or two. For the free water bottle someone might even give you a donation for the water bottles. Go buy multiple cases of water, two big round garbage containers or big insulated coolers, one table and multiple bags of ice. Place all the water in containers or coolers, empty all the bags of ice over the water bottles to keep the bottles cold and closed the lid. You are now ready to start your water bottle giveaway and don't forget to have your church logo wrap on each bottle for branding purposes. If you're not able to wrap the bottles with your church logo, make sure that you have flyers available to give out with all of your church, ministry or business information listed.

35.Clothing giveaway

Churches often provide free clothes to people who need and ask for them. Some churches hold clothing giveaways, where anyone can walk in, fill up a bag with clothes, and walk out. Most church clothing drives are geared toward the poor or homeless; this helps churches provide proper attire for people who need it. Church's' are an essential part of the lives of many people in our communities: they inspire and help the needy. Therefore, the clothes that they provide to their local communities can be so important, not just for those who might need them but also for those who donate them. By providing assistance with donation pickup and clothes distribution, churches and ministries can make it easier for donors to assist in their community without worrying about transportation, logistics, or accessibility.

Clothing to low-income people who can't afford to buy it from a store, especially during the winter season when the need for warm clothes is most urgent. Clothing Giveaway are free to everyone. People in your community don't need to donate clothes to come and pick out clothes. This a great outreach event where you can invite your neighbors and anyone else you think might benefit. You can even use a verse that says, "When I was naked you gave me some clothes"

36.Computer training

It is a common thing for children to work on computers, but some people are not well trained in using computers even for performing small activities. Particularly people like homemakers, senior citizens and those who are from the rural background, its hard operating a computer efficiently. Your church, ministry, or business can make available free computer training courses and computer repair classes for everyone! A computer training outreach can help many people with through-out your community and city improve their office skills, job attainment and advancement, develop marketable skills, increase earning potential, and enhance personal development.

37.Community Garden

If the church or a church member has an acre or more of garden-worthy land, you can put together a community garden. With plowing, planting, maintenance, and harvest, you're committing to a year-long project. You need someone knowledgeable to lead it and make sure you have a really good idea of what's needed:

- Volunteers
- Tools
- Plants
- Watering system and cost
- Fencing

A cultivated garden will connect your community together, and it can also provide some food for local shelters and food banks and food distribution centers.

38.Car Wash (Free or Donation)

Find a place with a good, central location with a water hookup for the car wash. Have some flyers or tickets made up for the car wash outreach with the location, date, day, and time of the car wash outreach event. Also, on the other side of the flyer you can have your church location and service times printed on the flyer. Now you're ready to distribute through-out the community and City.

39.Coffee mugs with your organizations name and logo printed on the mugs

Would you like to make an impact at your next church, ministry, business, or partnership meeting? Custom coffee mugs with your logos will help to get your message out. The combination of premium cups and coffee mugs with high-quality printing will deliver eye-catching results at your next community and city meetings.

40.Coffee Shop

If you have coffee connoisseurs in your congregation, a church sponsored coffee shop could be a great way to bridge your church with the community. Try offering coffee beans and coffee with a story. Depending on your church location, a coffee shop could be located on church property or in another area with high foot traffic. Perhaps an owner of established coffee shop will set aside one day a month for an outreach, such as "coffee for the community". Profits could be donated to a neighborhood need with church members volunteering their barista or waiter services.

41.Church Partnership

What's the difference between "Partners" and "Partnership"

Did you know that "Church partnership is powerful"? Your outreach efforts will be more effective when you are in partnership with other churches. You are also communicating through-out your community and city what church unity looks like. Sometimes churches are competitive, but they don't need to be. They should be service-oriented and if that means working together then cooperation should be welcomed. Church partnerships could include many of the activities on this list. Because your church is partnering, there may be bigger opportunities to impact your community.

42.Concert

Are there any Christian musicians, groups are choirs that are passing through your area? If so, consider hiring them for a concert. People love music and it's another easy opportunity to invite new faces to your church activity. Hiring musicians who don't have lyrics but are talented with instruments can make the event religiously neutral and attract both believers and non-believers.

43.Crossfit

Put the "cross" in CrossFit. Exercise and health play an important role in today's society. God tells us to treat our body as a temple, so exercise is a great way to follow Him. If you have exercise-minded members in your congregation, ask them about starting a faith-based CrossFit group. Work hard, reap rewards, and give thanks to God.

44.Dental Service (Mobile Truck)

Dental services can be delivered to rural communities through mobile dental vans or portable dental clinics in population centers, schools, or hard-to-reach areas. A mobile dental van may include the following components: working space, X-ray facilities, sterilization system, and computer. Unlike stationary dental clinics, mobile clinics provide greater physical access to dental care for medically underserved population in poor urban and remote rural communities and many existing dental clinics services at lower or no cost to the user. Services that are provided by mobile units include health screenings, dental services, or benefits enrollment. Dental services can be delivered to rural communities through mobile dental vans or portable dental clinics in population centers, schools, or hard-to-reach areas.

45.Dinner Party (Home or Church)

Have members of your congregation join and invite friends who are not currently attending the church. To make the event more engaging, consider selecting a volunteer to "host" each party. The host can then plan the menu and share the recipes with those that RSVP so that attendees can feel like they are truly sharing the same table.

46.Date Night for married couples

Most couples want to have a date night, but it often gets put on the back burner because of work and family responsibilities. Promote a community date night at the church where couples can converse, have a good meal, and have childcare taken care of on site.

47. Dinner for first Responders

First responders put their life on the line every day while serving our community. What is a first responder? A first responder is a person with specialized training who is among the first to arrive and provide assistance or incident resolution at the scene of an emergency, such as an accident, disaster, medical emergency, structure fire, crime, or terrorist attack. First responders typically include law enforcement officers, paramedics, emergency medical technicians, and firefighters. Appreciating local leaders and first responders is something everyone can agree on, and churches should celebrate them. Organize a barbeque at a public park, give out appreciation gifts, and thank your local leaders for their support.

48.Driving Lessons

Everyone is required to take driving lessons if they intend to drive on their own. If your church has qualified drivers, the church could provide driving lessons to hundreds of people each year. Put the name of your church on the side of the car and let the community know about this service. Drive safely!

49.Event Planning

Planning your next event can be as easy as 1, 2, 3! There are many ways that you can plan, through multiple websites online. Ray Hampton Outreach Ministries currently uses constantcontact.com Go online to find what works best for your Church, ministry, or business.

50.Emailing service

Statistics shows that emailing is a very effective tool that everyone can receive on their computer iPad or smartphone. To increase your email service just provide individuals with a keyword and text number. They'll immediately be added on to your e-mail list at your office, which means the days of writing it down on paper and losing or forgetting their email before you arrive to your office is over. This can be done by using a e-mail service.

51.Election Day prayer service

Plan a community-wide evening prayer service. This should be a totally agenda-free, non-partisan time (To be nonpartisan is to not be biased or partisan, especially toward any particular political group) for people in the community to gather and focus their attention on praying for the community and country. This can be a helpful outreach opportunity to build unity instead of division.

52.Easter celebration

On this day believers in Christ celebrate the resurrection of Jesus Christ this is also a day that you can invite your family and friends to enjoy not just a good service full of fun, food and fellowship but where they can also receive the word of God.

53.Easter EGG Hunt

1. Find a good, preferably gated, community space.

Whether it is someone's very large yard or a local community park. A gated space works best, because you don't have to worry about the safety of the children as they roam (to go from place to place without purpose or direction) the grounds. If you can't find a gated location, set clear boundaries to keep everyone in the right space.

2. Set the date in advance.

Start working early with your creative team to pick a date that works for everyone and coincides with your church or ministry calendar. Schedule the outreach event two weekends before Easter Sunday, so that participants can do family events or other larger events if they wish, and still get to participate in a community hunt.

3.Set ground rules for every participant.

Ask each family to donate at least a dozen eggs filled with treats. This way no one feels a financial burden, and normally people are very generous with several dozen donated. Each child then walks away with way more eggs than you would expect! Most children will hunt and receive nine to twelve eggs in their basket, so be prepared. If you're expecting one-hundred children, you will need 1,200 eggs.

4.Give yourself time.

Hiding 1200 eggs takes time. Don't rush yourself, set the egg hunt up early so that you'll have plenty of time to hide the eggs.

5.Set up age groups.

Allow the very youngest children to go first. Children under 3 are normally done "hunting" within 20-30 minutes. They maybe collect 10-12 eggs. Let the older children egg hunt after the little children have had their fun! This also greatly minimizes drama. If you are hosting older children, consider saving a few extra special eggs for them to search for. Place money and special prizes in multiple eggs, which are called the Golden Eggs

6.Bring extras.

Extra baskets or paper bags on hand are good for families who may expect them. This isn't strictly necessary, but it will help individuals and families who may have decided last minute to join.

7.Save your eggs.

If you plan to make this an annual event, save the eggs so you can use them the following year, when you host your next year's egg hunt! You might be surprised by how many eggs were unclaimed by children (They took the candy and left the egg). Don't throw the eggs away, just save them for next year!

Over one-thousand people attended our "Flashlight" Easter egg Hunt at Liberty Park in Renton, Washington to hunt for over fifteen-thousand plastic eggs filled with candy! G*o to YouTube and search for all the following Seattle International Church prepares for Egg Hunt at Liberty Park in Renton, Washington; Seattle International Church Flashlight Egg Hunt at Liberty Park in Renton, Washington Part 1; Seattle International Church Flashlight Egg Hunt at Liberty Park in Renton, Washington Part 2; Seattle International Church Flashlight Egg Hunt at Liberty Park in Renton, Washington Part 3* to check the Ray Hampton Outreach Ministries Egg Hunt Outreach.

54.ESL (English Second Language) Bible Study

If you have someone who is multilingual, host Bible studies for other languages for people whose English isn't too strong.

55. Education sponsorships

Education sponsorships to help children are common, but many of the most popular programs are for young students overseas. While those options are great, churches can also reach out to their community to assist with education opportunities. High school students might want to attend a Christian school but are unable to afford tuition. Similarly, university students could benefit from a scholarship. Assisting others with education is a wonderful outreach idea.

56.Food Truck

Food Trucks are great for any outreach event and can provide extra excitement especially when you bring in some of the most popular food trucks that are known through-out the city. You will automatically draw more attention and people to the outreach event. In the state of Florida where Ray Hampton Outreach Ministries east coast headquarters is located, food trucks are very popular. Food trucks can be a great option for locations that are hard to reach or that don't have a large kitchen or service area, and they are perfect for events that are outdoors. Before the food truck outreach event following are a few things you must do so the event can be successful.

1.Set a Budget

You will need to estimate the size of your crowd for the event and then contact several food truck vendors to get estimates. Some trucks may work with you on the menu and limit the selection to make service faster and to keep down costs.

2. Select your food truck

Choose a truck that compliments your theme or environment and the space you have to work with. Be careful to do your research so you know exactly what your truck looks like, if it plays music, and what it has to offer ahead of time. Your food truck can add to your desired ambiance and make it a party your guests will remember.

3.Select your food menu

Talk to the food truck owners about your event, your budget, how big your crowd will be, and how fast you want the people served. Consider if people will be sitting at tables, standing at tables, or walking around with plates, you want your food choices to be easy to eat and not too messy. Also consider special food for the children and ask your food truck vendor if they have food that is child friendly.

4.Select the best spot for the food truck

There are a few things to take into consideration when figuring out where to set up your food truck. First, you want it where it's easily accessible to your guests.

keep it close to the main action, without making it the focal point. Setting your food truck off to the side but close enough that everyone can easily get to it is smart. Plus make sure the location of the food truck doesn't interfere with the entrance and exits of your building and parking lot. Some cities have restrictions in place that determine where a food truck can be parked and at what times. You will want to check with your local city hall to find out your regulations and if any special permits or insurance are required.

5.Select an eating area

Part of your event atmosphere will be how you set up the area around the food trucks and where people will eat. A lot of this will be determined by where the food trucks are parked and your facility. If you have a grassy area you may want to put round tables and chairs there so the children can run around and play. If the sun is too hot or if there is a chance of rain, consider putting up canopies or offering shady or covered areas. Or if you are in climate where the weather can be questionable, you may want both outdoor and indoor areas.

High top style tables are also a great option, this way people can walk and talk as they move from table to table.

6.Selective timing

Be sure to talk to your food truck vendors about the timing of your event. You will want them set up and ready to go when your service ends. So have someone on your team be ready to greet them, direct them to the parking area and make sure they are ready for the crowd. Food trucks often cook everything to order, they can be slower to serve the food, so it would be a good idea to have music, games, performers, and other distractions for people to enjoy while they are standing in line or waiting for their order.

7.Spread the word

The goal of hosting a food truck or any other creative event is to draw more guest to your church. So, once you have your truck and event plans confirmed, you need to start spreading the word around your community. Most studies show that consumers need several "touches" before they will respond to an ad or marketing message, so that means you can't rely on just one method of communication. Here are some great options to look at:

Direct mail: The benefit of mailing out invitations to your community is that you can reach a large, but targeted area easily and quickly. Studies show that most people look at every piece of mail they receive So for a broad reach that can have a real impact, a postcard invitation is an inexpensive way start your marketing efforts.

Outdoor Banners: The reason you see so many billboards on the highway is because people really do read them. So, when you post a large outdoor banner outside your church it acts like a mini-billboard - promoting your event to passing traffic and reinforcing the message of your upcoming outreach event.

Personal Invitations: A personal invitation from one person to another is powerful. Most people are reluctant or shy about asking their friends and neighbors to come to church. One way to help empower the congregation is by providing them with invitation cards to hand out as they engage with others throughout the day.

Website & Social Media: Many of the visitors that are showing up to your weekly services will in most cases go online to look at your church website before they walk through your doors. You can't afford to ignore online guests and social media in your event planning. It's an inexpensive way to spread the word and an entirely new way to start conversations with people about faith. On your website, make sure your event and food trucks are promoted on your homepage with details on the service times and even information on the food that will be served. On social media, it's important to be part of a conversation and not just someone promoting an event. One idea is to have a poll asking people about their favorite foods or even about the trucks themselves. Also make sure the Food Truck is listing your location as one of their stops - ask them to include a link to your church's website too. Also encourage the congregation to share about the event with their social media friends.

Press Release/Publicity: Depending on the size of your community and what other things are going on, you may be able to get a local TV station to cover the outreach event. It's not every day that a church has food trucks outreach in their parking lot.

8.Get Help with Cleanup

One of the biggest advantages of a food truck catering an event is that cleanup is quick and easy. Food trucks use disposable paper plates and plastic cutlery. Many food trucks will provide receptacles so guests can just toss out their trash. Adding a few church volunteers for clean-up duties can help collect anything that's missed or left behind.

57.Fans to the homeless on extremely 'hot days"

For someone who is homeless in the summer heat, heat strokes, exhaustion, dehydration, violence, and serious illness are just some of the threats you face. It isn't easy. There are many ways you can help those experiencing homelessness in the summer heat. You can purchase hundreds of personal fans and keep them in your car. The fans can be a huge help to someone who is experiencing hot weather and doesn't have any air flow. The purpose is so they can cool off quickly.

57.Facebook (Meta)

You can create a Facebook group for your church, ministry or business and send them an invite by doing the following steps.

1.Go to facebook.com and create a like page for your organization.

2.Solicit twenty-five likes so that you can establish a "vanity URL" for your like page

3.Launch a group and keep it locked

4.Send an inbox invite to join the group to your new members using their Facebook address

5.Post a welcome message in the lock group welcoming each new member once they have accepted the invite

6.E-mail within seventy-two hours of the new members joining

58.Fundraising

It's time to put the word "fun" back into fundraising by having a successful mail or online department within your church, ministry, or business. Non-profit donations are very important for the life of the organization. Over ninety-five percent of every nonprofit in the United States accept donations through e-mail and other social media technology. I would like to ask you an important question, are you offering a way for people to donate online? Are you making it easy for people to make donations from their mobile device? The average nonprofit organization is either doing one or neither of these questions. I would like to show you three endeavors to increase your fund-raising campaign, such as how to put together a plan to let your supporters know about your campaign, why they should donate to your church, ministry, or business. How to execute your plan and how you can extend your organizational structure plan to have continued success throughout the year. All you would need to do to have an effective structure for outreach marketing is, an online donation page, and e-mails of individuals connected to your organization.

HOW TO PLAN YOUR DONATION CAMPAIGN

Before your church, ministry or business begins their donation campaign the planning strategy will be a very important foundation in getting it off the runway, to take off to its destination which means getting it in front of the right people. The following are the five-step process for arriving to the destination. What is the definition of the word step? It is a series of actions, processes, or measures taken to achieve a goal. Outreach marketing can be described as using a specific message to communicate between your group and the public for mutual benefit. This step-by-step process is intended to be used as a tool to help you create your own outreach fundraising strategy plan.

STEP #1. Setting your goals

Your goals should be unique to your church, ministry or business and your general statements should express a broad outreach focus. The goals and statements may include the increase of staff, paid or volunteers as well as building community recognition. Your objectives should be specific and measurable such as increasing volunteers, outreaches, or more financial support by twenty percent in the next six months.

What's your vision of success? Of course, you want people to donate but after the campaign has ended, what's specifically would make it a success? What is the dollar amount? What will these funds enable you to do that you're currently not able to get done? It is very important to write down your goals.

STEP #2. Understand your target group

Your target audience is the group of people you want to reach. Some criteria for defining your target audience may include age, parental status, ethnicity, homelessness etc. your mission statement will be very helpful in focusing on your target groups of people you want to reach. Keep in mind that not everyone has access to the same things. The aim is to meet each target group socially and economically. Different methods will always attract different people, but we'll have the same message. Lower income people often do not have access to the Internet so you would need to place flyers were inner-city and/ or suburban parents spend time, such as a laundromat, parks etc. remember "it's the message that is sacred not the method". Always make sure you provide a way for your target audience to receive additional information, through a telephone number, website, or place and meeting time. Remember, everyone may not have access to a telephone or computer.

Once you have thought about what you want to accomplish, you can shift your focus to the people you're trying to reach and a great place to start is with your supporters that have been financially given consistently daily, weekly, monthly, or even annually to the organization. Always keep a journal and write down the following answers.

Why do your biggest supporters, support your organization?

What is unique about the work that you're doing?

What has inspired your supporters to donate to your church, ministry, or business in the past?

Was there a particular fundraiser that exceeded your expectations?

What is the average amount your supporters generally give monthly, daily, or annually?

STEPS #3 Understanding your value

Your supporters have many churches, ministries, or businesses they can support so ask yourself the following three questions.

Why should they support my organization?

Who will benefit from the financial support of your supporters?

Why is your church, ministry or business asking for financial support?

STEP #4 How to Package your method and deliver your message

Now that you have a targeted group now you can assess the target group, and create the message. Now, it's time to determine the best delivery of your church, ministry or business message that has been packaged. Packaging can have many forms, including Flyers, a script using a phone tree or advertisement in a local newspaper. Brainstorm with the rest of your creative team about what form you want your message to take. Always keep in mind the resources that you may already have available in front of you for example, someone in the group may work at a place that will provide discounts for photocopying etc. Once you have decided what format will be best, decide as a team how to best prepare your message and method to get it out effectively. Remember, to always set deadlines for each task to be completed because it is not real until you write it down. Goals without dates are dreams, so start now!

STEP #5 Creating your financial support campaign

To create as a successful fundraising campaign, you will be using steps one to three which I previously discussed in how to plan your donation campaign.

Step number one which is setting your goals is one of the most important steps of creating your donation page, you will then use steps two to three to start drafting your church, ministry, or business donation page. Your financial supporters have many other organizations that they can support, but a question to ask yourself is.

Why should they support your cause?

Who will be benefiting from the financial support that you have been able to raise through your church, ministry, or business? For example, if you're church or ministry wanted to raise $5000 to provide gifts for children doing Christmas, to do this successfully you would first need to know the average donation from each of your financial supporters. Then you will also have to show your supporters how their financial generosity will be used because they are more likely to donate if they know the cause that they are financially supporting and the percentage toward the cause. Once you know your financial goal amount and what your average financial supporter gives then you can ask for a suggested donation of the average amount to meet your goal based on the amount of people on your list.

By evaluating your outreach marketing plan at the end of each outreach event you can determine what worked or did not work, and what adjustments need to be made for the future. There are many different tools to work your plan. Some messages will have obvious ways to measure results. For example, if you use the outreach plan to organize a winter coat drive, the number of coats you got back is an evident way to determine how successful you were, and so on. Meet with your creative team about how your results compared to your goal and how did they think people responded to your message and method and what needs to be changed to make it more effective next time.

The days of being stressful and the straining of raising funds are over it's time for you to put the word "fun" back in fundraising so you can work "smarter and not harder" By raising the funds you need for your project online. While you're sleeping people are giving online twenty-four hours a day toward your cause. If you plan the work, you can work the plan.

59.Family and friends' day

On this big day you can have everyone dress casually or wear a T-shirt with your church, ministry or business name on it or the theme for that big day. On this big day every member is encouraged to invite at least one guest and share with their guests that there will be multiple drawings and food served. On this big day there are multiple drawings of gift certificates to local businesses and special musical selections. Great idea for giveaways is Televisions, vacation package, grocery store certificates, dinner for one, two or for the entire family at their favorite restaurant, video game consoles, bikes and more this a great time for your creative team to be creative. On family and friends' day the greatest asset in your church, ministry or business are the members of your organization. Family and friends' day should be done at least four times a year (Once a quarter) and if scheduled more than four times during the year it will lose its excitement.

60.Financial Course

There are a lot of families who are suffering financially. They don't know how to make sound financial decisions, or they're crippled by credit card debt, or they're throttled by student loans—whatever the difficulty, they really could use some help! Financial classes are one of the best outreaches that the church, ministry or business can offer within your community and through-out the city. Financial literacy is part of being a responsible Christian and it's also a life skill that many people overlook. Online, you can find countless services that offer courses for a fee, but there are many free resources as well.

In your church there are responsible, finance individuals who know about managing money. Ask for volunteers to teach an introductory financial literacy course, which can be done over a weekend. Your community could benefit from the course and during the lesson you can discuss God's direction for managing money.

61. Foster care

Every Christian makes up the body of Christ. We all have different gifts and different passions and different burdens. We're all different parts of the body. That's important to realize in the foster care world as well. Not everyone is called to foster, not everyone is meant to foster, but I think everyone in the church in their own way can play their own part. Everyone with their own unique giftings can do something in regard to foster care. I think for some people maybe it's praying. For some people it may be supporting foster parents through their local Foster Parent Association or helping foster families within the church. Maybe when a family begins to foster, maybe it's taking them meals or taking them care packages. Asking, "what do you need?" "What can we buy?" "What kind of groceries can we buy or what size diapers do you need, wipes, or cleaning products?"

Teach about it on a Sunday or a series of Sundays, preaching about the gospel and God's heart for the orphaned and vulnerable. We're all not called to do the same thing but we're all certainly capable of doing something. Provide an opportunity for people in your church to gather and learn more about how to get involved with foster care - all the way from bringing children into their homes to serving and supporting those who do. Most churches celebrate child dedications during the year. Do the same for foster parents! Only bring the parents in front of the church and have the congregation pray over them and dedicate their support to them! Also, select a Sunday and invite social workers who are often overworked, underpaid, and severely underappreciated. Honor, encourage, love, and pray for all social workers that have been or currently involved with the families. Call or make a visit to local foster care agencies and ask if there are any specific needs, they know of that families have, such as general home maintenance, lawn care, car repair, etc. and encourage the congregation to take care of those needs. Your church can have volunteers or paid individuals to offer baby-sitting Services on a Friday or Saturday evening to allow foster families from the church and community the chance to have a date night!

Set a time on the church calendar and honor all the families by having a big party for foster families that attend the church and encourage them to invite other foster families as well. You can have bar-b-que at the park, or a appreciation dinner that shows them they are seen, appreciated, loved and supported. Child welfare agency offices often double as waiting rooms at all hours of the night for children waiting to be placed and parent/child visitation spaces. Ask if there are rooms that need makeovers and provide the materials and labor to create more welcoming and comfortable environments for the children. Children are often removed from their homes and placed in foster care with little to none of their own personal clothes or possessions. Find out from your local agencies what items that the children that are being placed need most and have your creative team organize volunteers to gather the items needed. Have a night of prayer dedicated to the children in foster care, the families they come from and the families that are caring for them now!

62.Food bank

Every city needs a good food bank. It should be open at least one day a week, to serve people that are experiencing food insecurity as well as build long lasting relationships through-out the community and city. Most of the work is connecting with local grocery stores and local businesses for food and financial donations. Starting a food bank outreach as part of your church, ministry or business is all about "serving others with your palms down and not your palms up".

63.Fair booth

Every year most communities, cities and counties have an annual fair. Setting up a booth for your church, ministry or business is a great way to engage with people that you normally wouldn't had met. Make sure that your booth has information about your organization and a free drawing for a special gift. Whatever you do just make sure that your booth is staff with friendly and fun people and the atmosphere is inviting. People will always remember their first impressions.

64.Father's Day celebration

A Father's Day celebration is a great outreach to have your church. Many churches have more women than men, so why not celebrate and honor the men in your church. There are at least four categories of men that attend your church

The Ones Who Are Fathers- Fathers who are raising their own children.

The Ones Who Stepped Up to be a father- Fathers who are raising children that are not biologically theirs (stepfathers, grandfathers, uncles, older brothers, foster dads, etc.).

The Ones Who Are Grieving- Fathers who are grieving the loss of a father, a relationship with their father, or a life lived with an absentee father.

Those Ones Who Want to Be Fathers- There are men who long to be fathers of their own. But for some reason, as of now it hasn't become a reality in their lives. There are many ways to celebrate the fathers on Father's Day. Getting the children involved in celebrating their dads at church is a great way to make Father's Day exciting. Have the children dress like their dads for church that morning for a fun photo opportunity. Create a special hand-made gift in children's church. Or have them fill out a questionnaire about their dads leading up to Father's Day and share some of the best answers with the congregation. Give out gifts to the fathers this might require some extra work, but it's definitely a great way to make men feel seen on Father's Day. Offer the dads in your congregation a gift, it could be as small as free coffee and a donut to start their Sunday or a Starbucks gift card with a father/dad's devotional book. This is also a great opportunity to acknowledge other men in your congregation. Whatever gift you offer, extend it to all men. This will allow you to include the men who are struggling to become fathers (a group that is so often overlooked), as well as anyone who is serving as a father!

Use your Sunday morning message this Father's Day to remind your congregation that no matter where they are in the journey of fatherhood, or what feelings they have about their own fathers, they have access to a God who is Father to all. This is a great opportunity to not only share this message with people who may have never heard it but also to encourage people in your congregation who are struggling without a father in their lives. Let them know that God is there to meet their "Father" need.

65.Free Haircuts

Did you know that your church can offer free haircuts to the community especially to families that are experiencing financial hardship. Just contact 10 local Barber shops within your surrounding areas and asked if they would donate a haircut to ten school age children. That's a total of one hundred children that will receive haircut before the first day of school.

66. Foot Care for the Homeless

Throughout the day, many homeless people either stand or walk. Their feet ache, and they go through sock after sock like a machine. As a result, the feet of many homeless people are exposed and in discomfort since they don't wear shoes. Whether it's chilly or raining, wearing thin or wet socks is a horrible experience. Having a variety of socks options is quite helpful.

67. First Aid Kit for the Homeless

You never know when a homeless person might need a first aid kit. They might have a simple cut or maybe a major cut. Either way, having a first aid kit handy can save the day in many situations and can be useful for homeless people.

68.Feeding the Homeless

Of course, food is top of the things homeless people need the most. Giving money to homeless people might be useless but giving them something to eat can help them right away. Besides, not every restaurant or business serves or welcomes homeless people. A homeless person will probably face discrimination, so why don't you just get some food and give it to them? Helping the hungry is one of the most common church outreach activities. It's a great way to serve others and improve the health of your community. Churches often work together to prepare large amounts of food and outreach can include Scripture, clothes, and toiletries. G*o to YouTube and search for the following Seattle International Church feeding the hungry* to check the

Ray Hampton Outreach Ministries feeding the Hungry Outreach.

69.Financial counseling

What is financial counseling? Financial counseling a one-on-one relationship to help guide an individual toward making financial improvements that meet individualized goals outlined by the individual and counselor. Anyone that lives in your community or city that is struggling with their finances in some capacity is a good candidate for financial counseling. They don't have to wait until their experiencing bankruptcy or foreclosure before they start financial counseling. Make sure that you have qualified people teaching the classes.

70.Greeters

Greeters who are paid or volunteer are one of the most important outreach teams in your church, ministry, or business. Why? Because individuals who are greeters will be the first people that will see new and/or repeat guest, members, or customers. Therefore, I personally would like to call all the greeters ministry, "First Touch".

71.Gas giveaway

For a one-thousand dollars you can provide gas for one-hundred vehicles for only ten dollars per vehicle or for fifteen hundred dollars you can provide gas for one - hundred automobiles for only fifteen dollars per vehicle.

Go to YouTube and search for all of the following 2010 Meet Me at The Pumps, Meet me at the pump Gas Give Away, Gas Give Away in Skyway to check the Ray Hampton Outreach Ministries Gas Give Away.

72.Grocery food bag giveaways

A grocery bag outreach is a great way to engage with individuals and families that are experiencing food insecurity. When putting together food bags make sure that all food items are nonperishable. Don't put food items such as fresh fruit, vegetables, and baked goods. Make sure that nonperishables aren't expired or about to expire and that the packaging is sealed. Canned vegetables, corn, peas, green beans and mixed vegetables, canned peaches, pineapple, fruit cocktail and canned juices as well. Many nonperishable, high-protein foods come in cans like tuna, salmon, sardines, shrimp, chicken, chili, baked beans, red beans, soups, and stews. Peanut butter is another nonperishable protein food makes a healthy choice. For your grains and Pasta, you can use dry foods such as rice and pasta which can go a long way. Add several boxes of macaroni and cheese dinners, spaghetti, and flavored rice mixes. Hot breakfast cereals such as oatmeal and grits are healthy nonperishables. Dry cereals that you can eat with or without milk are good choices, especially if you're giving to a family with children. Look for complete pancake mixes that require only water and add a bottle of syrup. Staples are very important in a grocery bag but don't forget to add some special treats, such as canned cranberry sauce, stuffing mix and pie filling. Nonperishable sweets such as chocolate, hard candy and cookies are greatly appreciated! Also, add nonperishable snacks like nuts, dried fruit such as raisins and apricots, banana chips and popcorn if they're in sealed packaging. If you know there's a baby in the family, be sure to include some baby food and powdered or canned formula. Finger foods for babies such as cereal and teething biscuits are also good additions.

73. Grooming Items for the Homeless

Items such as combs, brushes, razors, shaving cream, and nail care kits are very useful for homeless people. Just because they don't have a roof over their heads doesn't mean they don't need to groom from time to time.

74.Grocery store shopping carts

Everyone goes shopping! Every time someone place their food item in the shopping cart, they are looking at your advertisement. This advertisement is always placed on the inside or the outside nose of the shopping cart. I've been amazed by the amount of donations that Ray Hampton Outreach Ministries have received, because of our advertisement that says," $1.00 a day will keep hunger away". Keep it simple but effective so you can get the results you're expecting. The next time you go to the grocery store look at the sign on your shopping cart and call the advertising company to get your church, ministry or business advertisement started.

75.Grocery Shopping or pick up service

There are individuals that attend your church or lives in the community that are elderly or has a physical handicap that prevents them from going to the grocery store. A grocery shopping outreach ministry is a great way to engage with others that need this service. Grocery outreach is not church work, but it is kingdom work that will build long lasting relationships. "People don't care how much you know until they know how much you care"!

76.Golf

Golf is a fun way to encourage activity and build relationships. Organize the event and ask other churches to join for some friendly competition for community bragging rights. Invite church members and ask them to invite friends and family who don't attend church. This outreach can also be used to support a local cause in your community or city.

77. Gift Cards and Transportation passes for the Homeless

Gift cards are a great way for individuals and families that are experiencing homelessness to dine at a restaurant or go buy some clothing. Transportation passes can help the homeless move from one destination to another, so instead of giving the homeless money, make their lives easier with gift cards and transportation passes.

78.Handouts

Door hangers, Flyers, and postcards are an excellent way to communicate with others. Your five by seven postcards should be mailed ready with the return address already printed on the postcard. Postcards are a great way for individuals or families to see what your promoting but also everyone that's working at the post office can see what you're promoting as well, as your invitation or announcements travels to its destination. What is UV coating? UV (short for Ultra-Violet) coating gets its name from the process used to "cure" the finish on your printed materials. First, the UV Coating machine places a special coat of varnish to your printed materials, on one or both sides according to your preferences. UV coating is an excellent way to make your print marketing materials stand out: UV coating provides a brilliant glossy sheen to your business cards, postcards, flyers, and other materials. When getting your postcard printed use a glossy cardstock if you want the front of your card to really shine, for an extra cost you can have a UV coating put on it but it's not necessary, just make sure you do not put UV coating on the back of the card, why? because this is where the return address and stamp is located and when it is getting processed, the meter strip ink at the bottom of the card will smear and not permanently stick to the card. Also, when the information is printed on this side of the card leave an open space one inch from the bottom with no writing in this area this is where the mailing label will be so the machine will not detect any unnecessary writing that it thinks is the address.

79.Hygiene packs for the homeless

Poor hygiene is one of the major problems that a homeless person will have difficulty maintaining. Poor hygiene can cause a lot of diseases and infections. You can give away personal hygiene packs to the homeless. Hygiene packs should contain, but not limited to tampons, soaps, feminine pads, shaving supplies, deodorant, combs, brushes, clippers, files, hand sanitizer, sanitary wipes, toothbrush, toothpastes, socks, underwear and mouth wash are just a few of the essentials you'll need to create a male or female Hygiene Packs.

80.Hats for the homeless

Buy some hats to keep in your car. The sun can be brutal in the Summer or all year round in some states for the homeless, and a good hat would help to keep the sun off their head and face. If you would like to be creative, for a financial investment, you can have your organizations logo printed or embroidered on the hat. This would be a great return on your investment because you never know who might show up to one of your church services and say thank you!

81.Homeowners

You can send a postcard to homeowners to inform them about your church, ministry, or business. The postcard will welcome them into the community or city and congratulation on buying a new home. When a family moves into the community, their primary goal is to get settled and to do it quickly. They are searching to find new doctors, churches, home service providers and more. You can be the first to welcome them in the community which could enhance your church, ministry, or business. Even though most people use the four by six postcard which is very popular. I personally like using the six by nine postcards because it's bigger and it takes up more space in the mailbox and can be seen very easily. Postcards allow the new person to get a sneak preview of your church, ministry, or business without even stepping through your doors. One of the first things that most homeowners look for when moving into a new community is a church where their children can grow up and the family can enjoy. This is one of the first steps of a new family getting attached to their new community, that they now call home. It is very important that you only print answers to questions that people are asking or looking for on your postcard, such as the basic services that you offer. Don't put the history of your church, ministry, or business on the postcard they will only throw it away. There are data services that provides information all over the country about new homeowners. Once you designate your zip codes and your city that you would like to target, the data service will provide you with the data you need to reach your target audience. Because of the data services you now have saved a lot of time and thousands of dollars from doing the work yourself. Following are some items listed below that certain data services provide to help you grow your organization.

8. Name of the homeowner
9. Spouse name
10. Date of closing
11. Address
12. Sale price of new home
13. Mortgage amount
14. Estimated income
15. Down payment
16. Subdivision where home is built (if available)
17. Telephone number (if available)
18. Lender name
19. Sale Type (N= brand new home purchase and R=pre-existing home)
20. Seller name

Even though all this information is exciting news but the greatest of all is that it only cost a few cents per house to get this information and it can be shipped right to your office. Once you designate zip codes in your area data services will continue to send you new homeowner information each month until you call and cancel your order.

82.Home maintenance (Labor of Love)

If you have any qualified and certified maintenance individuals that attend your church or if you know of anyone that you could refer to someone in need of maintenance work, this would be a great "out of the box" outreach! Make sure anyone or business that you provide a reference for has great character and integrity!

83.Host a concert

Depending on your goals, hosting a concert can be a bit of a risk. You need to ask yourself if you intend to charge for the event, take a "love offering," or make it a free event. If you have local talent, you can negotiate the cost of getting them to come play or sing. This can be a great way to make your church a place that's known for supporting local artists. If you want to host a more well-known artist, you're probably going to need to make a significant commitment to pay for them.

84.Homecoming celebration

Why not put together a special service for all the church's former members? This can be a fun and meaningful outreach idea that can let your current congregation know the value you place on everyone that has worshiped with the church in the past. Invite back everyone that use to attend the church. This is an absolutely great way to connect the churches past, present, and future members together.

85.Hot coffee/chocolate (On a cold day)

This is an easy outreach. All you need is a table, container for the coffee or hot chocolate and of course the coffee or hot chocolate itself. Once all the items are in place you are ready to serve a hot beverage to everyone that engages. This is also a great time to engage with people that you normally would not have met.

86.Instagram

Instagram is a social networking app made for sharing photos and videos from a smart phone. Like Facebook or Twitter, everyone who creates an account has a profile and a newsfeed. When you post a photo or video on Instagram, it will be displayed on your profile. Other users who follow you will see your post in their own feed. Likewise, you will see posts from other users who you choose to follow. Set up an Instagram account for your church, ministry, or business. You can keep it private or public and use it to post pictures from outreach events, if your account is kept private only your members can view it. Get your outreach marketing out today by going to instagram.com.

87.Involvement with local Police Department

Every city and county have different requirements and application processes. Call your local police on Sherriff's department today!

88.Involvement with local City or County Council

Every city and county have different requirements and application processes. Call your local city or county council today!

89.Jail ministry

Volunteers are needed daily at jails and prisons. This outreach is powerful because you get to see lives transformed as the Gospel is being preached. Starting a Jail or prison outreach is one of the most effective ways you can directly impact the lives of incarcerated men and women.

90.July 4th (Independence Day)

Everyone enjoys a 4th of July fireworks celebration. If your church can budget the cost, consider putting on fireworks show for the community. Fireworks aren't cheap, but an outreach event like this can attract new guest to your church, especially children.

91.Childrens ministry

Does your Church have a children's ministry? Throughout my travels across the United States teaching on evangelism and outreach, I'm amazed at how many churches do not minister to the children. If there's not a ministry to the children, then there will be no feeder program to build a youth ministry. Therefore, community outreach is so important because if you don't have children growing up in the church and families coming into the church, then every member in weekly attendance is getting older, which means that your ministry or church is stagnate. No growth!

Starting a children's ministry can be a big challenge, but it's worth the challenge! You're working with parents and their children as well as providing relevant children curriculum. There is no one 'right way' to do a children's ministry. What worked in your children's ministry this year, will need adjustment next year. Like most ministry programs, children's church is always a work in progress. Having the right people in place from the beginning is essential. Who's going to lead the children's ministry, interested parents, and the pastor must be all in. You and the children's ministry team need to decide "What aged-groups of children will participate?" Many children ministries grade ranges from kindergarten to third grade. Others extend through the end of elementary school. You also need to determine where the preschoolers will go. Some churches have a class just for them during church, while others include preschoolers in children's church.

There are several important issues to be decided about the format. Will the children attend a portion of the adult service and then be dismissed? or Will the Parents check their children in at the children's facility before they enter the main sanctuary? Once the format and age-range are settled, you can now begin to choose the curriculum. Before you begin the children's ministry you have to Establish Discipline & Safety Guidelines, you will need to adopt some basic policies for safety and behavior management. If you are just starting out, begin with a simple one-page document. Plan a strategic meeting with your creative leadership team and create working guidelines. Post it in your room and make sure all the weekly children's church follows these guides. Decide the basic elements and general order you will follow. Place the guidelines for the children's ministry in a location where every parent and staff can see it and the children will also know what to expect. This will create consistency with your volunteer staff leaders.

Identify church members who has a passion for children and would make great leaders in the children's ministry. In order to keep the children's staff rested, plan a four-week volunteer rotation schedule for the children's church staff. It's important to let the church and parents know about the new children's ministry several weeks in advance. This is especially true if your congregation has never had a children's church. If you are in a small church, talk to all the parents' one-on-one. Be aware of any concerns that parents raise and ensure them that the program is optional for each family. Once you are a few weeks into the children's ministry meet with the children's leadership team to re-evaluate. Walk through all elements of your plan and talk about what is working and what is not working. When the evaluation is completed strategize on ways to improve the children ministry.

92.Laundry detergent for the Homeless

Just because someone is homeless doesn't mean they don't want to keep clean clothes. Giving the homeless laundry detergent will make a significant difference in the daily discomfort of someone who does not have a place to live.

93.Learning center

Did you know that your church can make a major impact in a child's educational process by starting a learning center in your community? This is the perfect outreach ministry! This is a great outreach to meet the needs of families that live in the community. Inviting children and families into a church-sponsored learning center would be a major help. Families want an environment where their children's total needs are met—spiritual, physical, emotional, and academic.

94.Library (Mobile Truck)

Did you know that the children in your community and City don't have to go to the library, but your Church, ministry or business can bring the library to them. Call the local Library and explain to them how you would like to partner with them to do an outreach in the community. G*o to YouTube and search for Seattle International Church and Dream Center summer feeding to children* to check the Ray Hampton Outreach Ministries Library Outreach.

95. Lunch Program for Children

Schools out for the summer and there are thousands of children that are going to be hungry looking for something to eat. While their parent or parents are at work trying to provide not only shelter but food on the table for their family. Your Church, ministry or business can make a Hugh difference by feeding the children in the daytime. G*o to YouTube and search for the following Seattle International Church and Dream Center summer feeding to Children* to check the Ray Hampton Outreach Ministries Children's Lunch Outreach.

96.Music Lessons

Most churches have a praise band, and all churches have a few members who can play an instrument, sing or both. If your church members have musical talents, you can start music lessons for ages. Parents are always looking for someone to teach their children music lessons.

97.Membership Marketing

One of the greatest ways to do membership marketing is to have the hospitality department schedule a welcome reception during the week. It's very important that the lead pastor/ general manager along with associates are in attendance. If there is a scheduling problem with the pastor/ general manager, then the welcome reception should be rescheduled until leadership representation is available. This will also allow the paid and volunteer staff of the church, ministry, or business two connect with the new members/clientele. If a person is paid or not, they are still staff. If they are a volunteer nobody knows but them, so their integrity is to work just like a paid staff, this is how promotion is given. Following are four very important things you need to have at your membership marketing event.

Food-It's not necessary to have a complete dinner at the event, but finger food appetizers will be acceptable, remember you're not there to eat you're there to build long lasting relationships with the new members/clientele.

Music-A full live band is not necessary, you can keep it as simple as having music playing in the background which will not overwhelm or devalue the moment but will add value to the moment.

Gifts-Everyone loves to receive a gift. It's a great idea to have a drawing for special gifts to local businesses in the community for the new members/customers to use.

Photographer-Set up a red carpet with a nice background and have a photographer take pictures of the new members/ customers along with the staff if they would like.

98.Membership Retention

Every time a person makes a visit to your church, ministry, or business they are no longer a visitor, but they are now known as a guest. Your goal is to get connected with the guest. To not connect is to disconnect. Following are some key points to keep membership/ customer retention.

1.It's very important that the pastor/manager personally calls each new member/ customer and if it is too time consuming to make a "live call". If time doesn't permit to do a live call, then use a calling system, which is a prerecorded message to call the new member/ customer. The phone calls should take place within 24 hours!

2. If there is a dedicated and/ or appointed individual to contact the new members/ customers within the church, ministry, or business they should call

them as well, but remember, that it is imperative that the first voice they hear is from their new pastor/ manager.

3. Each new member/ customer should receive a personalized welcome letter by e-mail and a personal letter by regular mail within 48 hours.

4. Have someone from the hospitality department make a home visit (If possible) within 72 hours. Upon arrival present the individual or family with a gift that they will be able to use. Remember, it is important to be very sensitive to the needs of the household before visiting.

5. When looking at the ministry/department interest that was listed on their new members/ customers form have been reviewed, the leader of that ministry/department needs to send the individual/family a welcome e-mail within seven days and make sure the welcome e-mail states the meeting schedule and any requirements to be part of that ministry/department.

6. The assistant administrator/manager of that ministry/department that the new members/customers are involved in should call the new members/customers within 14 days to make sure they are starting to get connected not just to the church, ministry, or business but to some type of involvement within the church, ministry, or business. Remember, this is a process so be very sensitive to the new member/customer so don't try to rush them, just be patient.

99.Mail (Bulk Mailing)

Did you that you can mail out a letter to every current resident in your city. One of the first things you must do is get your nonprofit mailing status approved and then go to a title company to request the addresses in the area that you desire to reach. With your 501C3 status you can mail a letter for less than a third of the price of a regular stamp. Go to or call your local post office today for information to get started!

100.Mid-week service theme

Is there a local, national, or international event that has really impacted your city? Plan a mid-week evening service with themed worship and a relevant message. It's amazing how many people will come to church when they're going through a difficult or confusing time.

101.Movie night at your church

Does your church or ministry have a great audio/visual setup and people that are trained to run it effectively? Would you like to use it for showing movies? This can be a weekly event that happens all summer or all year! If you live in a college town, a movie night followed by a discussion about its themes and characters can be an interesting way to bring people into your church. You might be surprised by the suggested financial investment and time commitment here, but this isn't an idea you want to get into unless you're willing to invest in the proper non-theatrical public performance license which can be pricey (dependent upon what kind of movies you plan on showing). If you're going to invest in a license, you might as well make family movie nights a regular event. I still remember movie nights at my church. It was an opportunity for families to enjoy a great movie with other families. It also provides a free form of entertainment outside the home. Organize outdoor movies using blankets and projector and screen. This is particularly great if you live in a climate where evenings are warm and comfortable.

102.Movie Theaters (Advertisement)

Can you imagine eight movie screens in a theater that shows four movies a day that means that your advertisement is shown thirty-two times a day, which will be seen by thousands of captivated people while they are eating popcorn, hot dogs in drinking soda. This is so amazing because it is "network marketing by attraction" you are building the first step of network marketing without even being there.

103.Mother's Day celebration

On Mother's Day show a video during church service of the children sharing stories why they love their mom. Give a special Mother's Day gift to all the moms in your congregation. A few examples could be Flowers, Gift cards to a local coffee shop or restaurant, a new journal, books, coffee mug or tumbler, a cookbook, lunch, or breakfast where the moms don't have to cook or clean at all! They'll be blessed with great food and enjoy it even more without having to prepare, cook, or clean it up. Receive a special Mother's Day offering that goes towards a ministry that supports moms and children in your community. Create a chocolate or candy buffet that all moms can enjoy! Provide a nice photo backdrop and take pictures of families together on Mother's Day. They can have somebody take a photo for them from their phone, they can take a selfie, or you can bring in a professional photographer. Then, collect email addresses and email the photos to them directly. In children's church have teachers create a church Mother's Day card and gift that they can give to their moms. During your service, play or have your worship team sing a special Mother's Day song for church. Even though Mother's Day should be a day of celebration, and you should go out of your way to bless moms during your church Mother's Day service, it's also a hard day for many. Mother's Day can be very difficult for people who have recently lost their mom, are having fertility issues, have experienced miscarriage, or don't have a good relationship with their mom. Don't ignore this, instead acknowledge the pain and be ready to minister to those who need it. It may also be a wise idea to celebrate all women in your church in general, and not just single out the mothers. After all, women do tend to care for those around them even if they don't have the official title of "mom." This could also eliminate extra pain or make some feel left out.

104.Mother's morning out

This outreach is during the morning and early afternoon hours, to provide mothers an opportunity to get out and get some items accomplished without having to bring their child/children. Make sure that you have a well-defined start and stop time. This consistent outreach could also grow your children's ministry/church.

105.Meal preparation for the community

A community meal is a great time for gathering together with a group of people in order to share food and time together. As Christians, we gather together to eat, both with people we know and people we don't know, why? because Jesus did. If you read through any of the Gospels, you will find Jesus eating with all kinds of people, in all kinds of situations. Jesus eats in homes, Jesus eats with crowds, and Jesus eats with his close friends. In all of those situations, Jesus is sharing the good news of the gospel by being present with people, by engaging in some of life's most basic and essential activities with them, and by spending time with them. If we follow Jesus's example, we'll probably be part of all kinds of community meals too. Food ministry is as wonderful a way to share the gospel and build community relationships. Following are a few examples of a community meal; Lunch after Sunday service, Neighborhood block party where you will encounter people that you've never met, Gathering with a small group for dinner and fellowship at your home. Any way that you gather people together and share in eating some good food is a "community meal."

What makes a great community meal is first class hospitality.

When a host takes time to think about the meal in advance, to consider who is coming and what they might need to feel welcomed, comfortable, and safe and what you can as a church to create a great atmosphere for everyone. First class hospitality takes time, and you must know what questions to ask to plan well.

Below, are a few of questions to help you engage with first class hospitality as you plan for a community meal, and some of the details that go with them. Key questions to ask yourself when you plan a community meal. Think about the group you're hosting. Are they members of your church? Members of the community? Do you know them personally? Will they be bringing guests or family members? Knowing who you've invited can help you think about what they might need. For example, will families need highchairs? Do you know how many people will come, or do you need to set out extra chairs? Consider how people will hear you if you are doing any kind of speaking. In large groups or spaces (like a church fellowship hall, cafeteria, or parking lot), always use a microphone. Even if you are simply giving directions to the food and offering a prayer, using a microphone will allow everyone, especially anyone who is hard of hearing, to hear and understand you. Even if you have a loud voice, don't assume that everyone will be able to hear you.

How will you address food allergies or restricted diets? It is so important and often overlooked. There are a lot of people today who have food restrictions, allergies, or modified diets. These might be personal choices, but they might be related to serious medical conditions. And, they might not be known to you, even if you know someone well. If you want to create a safe space for people to eat together, don't discount the importance of this issue. It could literally be a matter of life or death for some people. A lot of community meals have potlucks or buffet style food lines. This can be great, because you get a lot of different dishes so, and everyone can find something they like. However, you need to think about people who have allergies or people who have food restrictions. You and your guests might not know who has food restrictions or what they are, so think about how to let people know what is in food, so that they can feel safe in making wise choices. Labels and ingredient lists are great idea to have next to the food item. Don't make people ask what is in a dish! The people serving the food might not be the people who made the food, so they might not actually know what the ingredients are. Consider providing a few options that meet the needs of the most common food restrictions.

Providing dishes that are vegan (vegetarian and dairy free), gluten free, and nut free make events much more welcoming, especially if you let everyone know that these options are available! Watch out for cross contamination. If you have gluten-free food, especially, make sure that it is not on the same plate as food containing gluten. Give gluten free rolls their own basket, with a cover. Make sure that each dish has its own serving utensils, so that people aren't transferring food from one plate into another dish.

It is important for people to feel welcomed. Make sure to have someone that is friendly and hospitable to greet people. If you have a group that already knows one another, whether it is your congregation or a group of friends, make sure you encourage them to engage with people that they have never met. Nothing is more disappointing than coming to a "community" gathering and not having anyone sit with you or engage you in good conversation. Remember to encourage people to sit with someone they don't know or haven't seen in a while so everyone will feel welcome!

106.Medical (mobile truck)

Another crucial service that many low-income areas need is quality healthcare and medical services. Hosting a mobile medical outreach directly to people in need will help eliminate some of the barriers they face in accessing healthcare. A mobile medical outreach can offer a unique opportunity to reach communities directly in a convenient and self-contained environment when transportation is an issue of going to have a health checkup. Your church or ministry can bring the clinic to the community and be known as, "The Church that cares".

107.Mentorship programs

Have you ever thought about starting a mentoring program children, youth, or adults at your church? Very few people today come to know Christ on their own—it usually happens in relationship. Maybe it was a parent, friend, or a combination of several people who helped you understand who God is and how to grow in him. A mentoring program provides a great and effective way to help others have accountability as they continued to be discipled and grow in God's word. Although mentoring programs is time consuming, it's well worth the investment.

108.Neighborhood Marketing

Have you ever said to yourself, I wish I could meet people throughout my community? It is important to build relationships with those within and around your communities or at least know who they are. Even though there might be a few people throughout your community that rather be disconnected and isolate themselves. Remember, there are hundreds of individuals and families that are waiting to be connected but they are waiting to hear from you. Have you been waiting a long time for a certain individual to call you and the reason why you don't call them is because they don't ever call you and finally one day you said to yourself, I'm just going to call them. When they finally answer the phone, you can hear the excitement of happiness in their voice that you have called them. You probably were in total shock once you heard the excitement of their voice over the phone. Be honest, were you prepared to say to them, "why haven't you called me" and your response probably going to be, "I wasn't calling you because you weren't calling me" isn't it amazing how two minds can think the same thing but never meet. Well, you don't have to wait any longer instead of being disconnected from people within your community you can be connected to them on purpose. With only a few clicks on your computer you can meet the person down the street, if they have already joined the following website and if not, you can personally invite them to sign up and always be ready to support each other's events. Are you ready to start building relationships today just go to nextdoor.com

109.Nursing home ministry

Growing up, my family always visited a nursing home for seniors, I remember my grandmother having us sing songs as a choir to entertain not just the seniors, but staff enjoyed it as well. We socialized with the people living there and the people were appreciative because they rarely had family visit them. I remember how their eyes were full of joy when they saw younger people (they were usually only around other seniors, doctors, and nurses). Regular nursing home visits are a great opportunity for your church to make a difference in a community. All ages can get involved with a nursing home ministry.

110.Newsworthy Marketing

Contact your local news station when you are one week away from any of your major outreach events and let them know that the outreach event that is getting ready to happen is a BIG DEAL! Let the media know that the outreach event is going to have a major impact throughout the community and city. Once the media shows up you are going to have to be organized its vitally important to be prepared to deliver what you said you would do. It is always a great thing when talking to the media to "under promise but over deliver" remember that your promise must be big which will make your delivery even bigger. The news media will not stay around for something that is not newsworthy their time is too valuable to be playing games so unless you are sure you have a major outreach event, I would wait to call them. Always remember that what might be important to you, might not be valuable to them. Just ask yourself the following question before you called the media; What is our church, ministries, or business competitive advantage? Just in case you might be wondering what the words competitive advantage means: A competitive advantage is a condition or circumstance that puts a company in a favorable or superior business position; Expansion is vital to maintaining a competitive advantage. As you continue to keep your consistency you will grow causing your church, ministry, or business to become bigger, better, and stronger than before.

111.New Year's Eve Celebration

New Year's Eve is one of the most fun times of year. If we look back at our lives, we can likely recall where we were for most New Year celebrations. Some people enjoy visiting the big city for New Year's Eve, while others prefer staying home with family. So why not do something in between? Invite kids or adults to a safe and wholesome New Year's celebration. Include music, movies, and food.

112.Online Course

If you would like to create online courses, I have a few questions to ask you. Are you tired of not having enough money to rent out a space to teach others what you have been born to do? Do you have a dream? What are you willing to give up for your dream? Is your dream bigger than you? Maybe there is something that is between your dreams and your destiny, and it can be as simple as a few clicks away to expand what you have been given to expose to others. I believe that you were born to teach and encourage others, how to effectively engage with others, be equipped, empowered for evangelism and outreach. You can teach and show thousands of individuals across the United States how to do the work, that have been given to you. I have some good news for you, are you ready? You can upload your videos for online courses and allow people to step into your virtual classroom from all over the world by enrolling today at udemy.com I want you to always remember that "the promise of your prosperity is always connected to your passion".

113. Painting houses in the community

Do you currently have qualified painters that attend at your church or are you in partnership with any painting companies? If you answered yes, you could have a conversation with them about volunteering their time and materials to help improve their community? Identify a neighborhood where there are homes that need painting. In many cases you'll find that single parents or seniors don't have the time or resources to do the job themselves. Painting a few homes in your community will improve the neighborhood, make the neighbors happy, and increase property values. It's a win-win for the church and community.

114. Professional Sporting Event

If you've been to a sporting event, you've probably seen large non-profit organizations mentioned on the Jumbotron (A Jumbotron sometimes referred to as jumbovision, is a video display using large-screen television technology). Non-profit organizations can buy entire sections of seats at a discounted price or sometimes the tickets are even donated, and everyone will enjoy a day of sports. Your church can even have a tailgating party in the parking lot of the stadium and engage with people that are passing by. Bring a sign of your church and wave it during the game – you never know, you might be on television!

115.Parental Classes

Prenatal classes are something most expecting mothers and fathers participate in. The classes are designed to build confidence and physical resilience during the birthing process. If you have the expertise in your church, consider organizing free prenatal classes and use it as a tool for outreach.

116. Parking Lot

As individuals and families arrive on the premises of the church, do you have parking lot attendants prepared to greet and serve them as they are preparing to get out of their automobile? Once their car comes to a complete stop, you can begin by opening their door and assisting them out of the vehicle. On a rainy day you can even provide umbrellas as your walking with them to the church entrance. In some cases, you can even offer valet parking. This is a nice first touch for your church, ministry, or business.

117. Pillows for the Homeless

Many people can hardly sleep without resting their heads on a pillow, can you imagine how difficult it would be for someone to sleep on a hard floor without a pillow. Individuals and families that are homeless experience this issue daily not being able to have the comfort of a pillow. Have you ever thought about collecting "pillows for the homeless". Plan a Sunday were everyone brings a new pillow or multiple pillows to church. Once the pillows are all in plan a Saturday outreach and go through-out the community/city and give a pillow to the homeless or donate them to your local shelter.

118.Podcast

Have you ever thought about uploading your effective teachings onto the Internet? The Internet connects to millions of people and has enabled almost anyone with a computer to log on to a podcast. Podcasting allows virtually anyone with a computer to hear great teachings. Log on to one of several podcast sites on the web, and you can download content ranging from music, sports, and great teachings on a variety of topics. Podcasting is a digital audio technology to create an almost endless supply of content. Podcasting is a free service that allows Internet users to pull audio files "typically MP3" from a podcasting website to listen to on their computers or personal digital audio players. The term comes from a combination of the words iPod "personal digital audio player made by apple" in broadcasting. Even though the term is derived from the iPod, you don't need an iPod to listen to a podcast. You can use virtually any portable media player on your smart mobile phone or computer.

Unlike Internet radio, users don't have to tune in to a particular broadcast. Instead, they download the podcast on demand or subscribe via an RSS "really simple syndication", which automatically downloads the podcast to their computers. Download the podcast app today to your smartphone and be able to listen to millions of people around the world or start your own podcast account and upload your own recordings and have people listen to you, this is an excellent way to market your outreach efforts, there are many other applications for podcasting just turn on your smartphone and search for podcasting apps or go to podcasts.com and get started today the world is waiting for you!

119.Phone calling

The days of calling one person at a time is over, can imagine having to call everyone that you meet throughout the day and week to remind them of upcoming events that you're having. There is not enough time in the day for you to accomplish this task effectively. Did you know that "one phone call will do it all". Instead of trying to reach the thousands and not connecting to the one, now by connecting to the one you can reach the thousands. For approximately only a small amount of money you can reach hundreds of people if not thousands. It will only take you ninety-seconds to reach thousands. This can be accomplished by using a phone calling service.

120.Phone App

Phone apps are another great outreaching tool because everyone that has a smartphone uses mobile phone apps. Mobile phone apps can give an individual all the information that you would like them to know about regarding your church, ministry, or business. Mobile apps are very simple to navigate, to begin the individual needs to download your mobile app to their phone and when the download is completed, they will be able to see every current and upcoming outreach event that your church, ministry, or business will be doing in your community, city, the United States, or the world! The following are just two impactful ways a mobile app can add immediate value to your organization.

You can increase your visibility by millions which means that most churches, ministries, or businesses experience more downloads than people within their organization which will not only cause growth of outside exposure but expansion of your inside as well.

You can receive significant increase by your daily financial contributions by having an easily accessible place for anyone to give through their phone app

There are so many mobile apps that are available on the market today and growing daily that it would be impossible for me to list and keep up with all of them in this book title “out of your seat on your feet and in the streets”. If you know of any mobile apps that will enhance outreach marketing, send an e-mail to rayhampton@eachonereachone.net

121.Parent night off

Why not open the church up as a daycare on a Friday or Saturday night, and allow local families to drop off their children so they can go out and have a child-free date? All you need is a couple of adults, some teenagers, snacks, and activities to keep the children occupied. Remember, this is an outreach, so don’t let it become a service you’re only providing for church members. Encourage people in your church to use this an opportunity to double date with couples who don’t attend. This is a major outreach because the new couple get to have an awesome experience with the church, but they also have an opportunity to spend the evening building a closer relationship with church-member friends.

122.Preachers in the park

Street evangelism doesn't only mean approaching strangers. Sometimes it's better to let them approach you. Create a "booth at a park" or on a busy walkway. Have a sign that describes your church and your purpose.

123.Prayer booth

Have you ever thought about having your church set up prayer booths around the city? A prayer booth is an expression of your church's love for their community and city. As people visit the prayer booth, they will often share a current need. They will stay as long as they want or feel comfortable doing. I don't recommend setting up a prayer booth inside the church if you're having an outdoor outreach event, because it is out of the traffic pattern of the people who are attending the outreach. When people are walking, riding their bike, on the bus or driving down the streets, they will always notice your prayer booth signage. Most people that are going to stop by the booth are unbelievers that are going through a crisis. Remember, your not there to talk about your church , you are there to pray (After prayer you can give prayer information along with church information). The ultimate goal of the prayer booth is to show them how "Christ can take care of the crisis".

124.Prayer Groups

Prayer groups and small groups are usually reserved for regular church attendees. Your church can also organize prayer breakfasts and community prayers at public parks. You can also offer prayers to community leaders, schools, and families. When your organizing prayer groups it's very important that you, "Think outside the box".

125. Pet food for the Homeless

It shouldn't come as a surprise that homeless people have pets, too. Well, they do, and just as they need to survive, they also need to feed their pet. For homeless people, having a pet can be a lifesaver because, most of the time, they abandon their friends and family. But their pet serves as a friend to them. Think about having the congregation bring a bunch a pet food, for dogs and cats to church on a Saturday morning and go find some homeless encampments and bless their pets by donating pet food today!

126.Pre-school/Kindergarten

Many churches offer preschool and kindergarten services. Church members who have teaching backgrounds or experience with babysitting may volunteer their time to help others. A fee could be charged to help raise money for the church and it could attract parents who want a safe, faith-based place to teach their children.

127.QR Codes

QR code which is the abbreviation for “quick response” code was first design for the automotive industry in Japan. A barcode is a machine-readable optical label that contains information about the item to which it is attached. A QR code stores the data to which it is connected to. The QR code system became popular outside the automotive industry due to its fast readability greater storage capacity compared to standard UPC barcodes. Applications include product tracking, item identification, time tracking, document management, and general marketing. A QR code can be read by a smart phone with a camera, the cost is free to download and create a basic QR generator to your smartphone and once it is created you can print it out and place it on several items such as on your business card, automobiles, clothing, banners, and stationery. Once the person scans your QR code it will take them directly to your church, ministry, or business website.

128.Queen for a day (Self-Care)

Have you ever thought about honoring a woman that attends the church? Is there’s a woman in the church whos’ been experiencing financial problems and having difficulty with self-care? You can choose her to be a "Queen for a day". What's a Queen for a day? It's when you're providing a pedicure, manicure, hair salon, home makeover, dinner (at her favorite restaurant) etc. Whatever you do be very creative leaving her with a WOW Factor!

129.Referral Cards

Keep your church or ministry referral cards on hand in your wallet and pass them out as you come across someone in need. This tells someone where they can go to get out of the heat, find a meal, a place to stay, and a place to transform their life.

130. Reusable containers for the Homeless

These containers can receive food at homeless shelters. Remember, food is one of the basic things every human needs to survive. Homeless shelters usually pass out food to those who can't package that food for later. Reusable containers can help a homeless person to store food and to eat later.

131.Restaurants Tour Group

Your church could organize a food group that meets each month and visits restaurants and food trucks in the community. They could review the food and help the community know which places serve the best food!

132.Radio

AM stations are not bad they just have a weaker signal strength than FM, most people listen to popular stations on FM this is where you should do your advertisement or broadcasts. Depending on your target audience make sure that your advertisement is relevant to the listeners that you are trying to reach. For example, if you want the young rhythm Blues listeners ask the station for print out of their listening audience.

133.Raise money for a local cause

There is a lot of local cause in your community and city. Whenever your church starts to raise money for one of them, that is an outreach. Not only are you in the community raising money and awareness for a local cause, but you're also communicating that your church is committed to the needs of the community. Make sure that you have someone that is knowledgeable on project management, fundraising, and marketing before you decide to raise money for any cause. Empower people to donate online or on their mobile phones at any time, regardless of whether they have cash on them or if they can attend a weekly service.

134.Recognition service

If there's a charity, ministry, service, or business doing amazing things for your community or city, recognize them in a special service. Let them know you're planning a service in their honor. With enough notice, many from the organization will attend. Maybe you can even take up a special offering for them! This service could be for students who have led an important fundraiser or volunteered at a charity event, the staff at a local soup kitchen or homeless shelter, or a business that has developed a reputation for giving back.

135.Recovery groups

If your church has the room for it, consider letting recovery groups use it during the week. There are all kinds of groups that would benefit from using your facility like:

- Alcoholics Anonymous
- Narcotics Anonymous
- Divorce Recovery
- Eating Disorders Anonymous

Your church can play a pivotal role in their ability to get better and will likely provide an opportunity to get to know people who need to meet Jesus. As a bonus, the visiting group members will become familiar with your church building's layout which will make them a little more comfortable when they show up on Sunday morning.

136. Rain Gear for the Homeless

This is self-explanatory. Weather and climatic changes have no respect for anyone, including homeless people, so if you want to make their lives easier, get some rain gear such as umbrellas, rain coats and any other rain proof gear and go give it to the homeless that are living in your community and city.

137. Seasonal wear for the Homeless

Did you know that your church can give out cool wearing clothes to the homeless for the summer and if it's the winter, warm clothes for the. Clothing items such as; hats, tank tops, t-shirts, shorts, slacks, sweat pants, sweat shirts, jackets, sweaters, hand warmers, gloves and socks, new underwear and etc.. The change of seasons is something many people don't think about giving to homeless shelters. The right clothing will really help homeless people wear clothes according to the season.

138. Social Media

A social media outreach is the perfect opportunity for your church to meet people in their times of need or providing answers to their big questions by sharing the gospel.

As believers in Christ, we have all been called to go make disciples. How effective can your outreach be if you could reach a much wider and bigger audience or community by using social media? Social media is definitely a tool that can be used to enhance evangelism and outreach if used correctly and can bring a community closer together.

139.Super bowl party

The Super Bowl is one of the biggest events of the year, and it can be a wonderful opportunity to have individuals and families visit the church, but it must be done correctly. Most people would prefer to watch the Super bowl at home or with close friends, so there needs to be some real thought put into how you'll attract people. Not only will you need a commitment from your congregation to show up themselves (and invite their friends), but you might also want to invest in some items to raffle off. This raffle can be done during the halftime show. Make sure that your game food ready with such items like; Hotdogs, potato chips, can or bottle soda, hamburgers, fries, popcorn etc. Be creative!

Most of your investment money will go into creating invitations, buying snacks and food, investing in some great raffle items (you can probably get donations or discounts from local businesses, too). Make sure you know what the NFL expects from churches sponsoring such an event.

140. Sunscreen for the Homeless

There are some homeless people who go unnoticed. It can get very hot in the summer and people can get burned. Homelessness has long-term consequences to their health, which is why it is so important for people that are experiencing homelessness get housing as soon as possible. As the congregation is dismiss encourage each person take some sunscreen with them (Have a container full of sunscreen by the exit doors or have the greeter team handing them out). The homeless will thank you for it!

141.Senior Center

Senior Center is another outreach idea that's more about investing in the community than it is about getting an immediate return on your outreach. There are several ways you can invest in local senior centers:

- Lead worship services
- Serve meals at breakfast, lunch and or dinner
- Visit with seniors
- Stock the facility with resources like books and movies

Not only can you really minister to the seniors in your community at a time in their life when they feel left out, but you also get to teach your congregation how to serve others. Your outreach will affect the lives of the senior center's staff and family members of the residents.

142.Sponsor a school classroom

If you really want to make an impact in your community, invest in a school or a classroom. This can include purchasing of supplies, volunteering as helpers or chaperones, or maintaining the grounds or equipment. To get the most out of this outreach idea, you'll have to commit to something long-term. What you can expect from sponsoring a school or classroom is a strong reputation, trust, and influence. You'll be building important relationships with the staff and community. When you've established trust, you can almost guarantee that they'll come to you with information about families that need help and assistance. It's like you're creating a perpetual outreach.

143. Sport League

Do you have any land that's available or a gym at your church? In larger cities, space might not be available. However, in rural areas, churches often have extra land that can be used for games and events. If your church is paired with a school, there will likely be a gym for basketball and volleyball. Organize a sports league where people from the community can compete and exercise. Volleyball, indoor soccer etc. are fun ways to compete that don't require too much land or space. If your church doesn't have space, consider partnering with a church that does. One of the easiest ways to reach your community outside the church is to build relationships. Sports are a great way to start relationship building!

144.School supplies giveaway

Make an announcement to the congregation, that you would like them to donate money towards buying school supplies or you can challenge each one of them to bring school supplies to each service they attend and place the items in the barrel or box that has been provided.

- Once you have supplies, you can:
- Donate the items to a shelter or organization
- Donate the items to a school to give to children who need the supplies
- Set up a little "store" in the church and allow people to buy the supplies at discounted rates so they don't feel like they're receiving handouts
- Invite the community or even the whole city to a school supplies giveaway

145.Street Ministry

Have you ever walked up to a person on the street and chatted with them? It takes courage and may be uncomfortable, but most people are open to a conversation if it's respectful. Street evangelizing doesn't only mean approaching strangers. Sometimes it's better to let them approach you. Create a booth at a park or on a busy walkway. Have a sign that describes your church and your purpose. Offer a few store-bought snacks and you'll be surprised how many people stop to learn more about your mission.

146.Self-Defense

Self-defense is important for everyone. Men, women, and children should be able to protect themselves and their family. Martial arts can provide your congregation and community with confidence and strength. A self-defense class doesn't have to be a long-term commitment. Introductory classes could be offered to the community by members of your congregation who regularly train. Physical activity is a great opportunity to share a message of faith. Local law enforcement agencies often offer classes at low cost or free. You could host them at your church.

147. Socks for the Homeless

Homeless people are always on the move. They really take off their shoes, and that is because they always have to keep changing from one location to another. If you're going to be helping a homeless person, one thing homeless people need the most is socks. They need to wear them with shoes, and it can help warm their feet.

148. Shoe giveaway to Children

Have you ever thought about hosting or having a shoe giveaway to children at your church? This outreach event can be accomplished when children are out of school for the summer and called "Summer shoe give away for children" or you can do the outreach event when its time for the children to return to school called "Back to school shoe giveaway". Your church can help thousands of children step back into school in style.

149. Shoes for the Homeless

Just like socks, shoes are also very important for individuals and families that's experiencing homelessness. They need something comfortable to wear when walking around. If you're going to be helping a individual or family that is homeless, yes socks are important but they would feel a lot better if they were worn with a pair of shoes.

150. Toy Give Giveaway

Would your Church, Ministry or business like to give away 500 toys or even 22,000 toys for Christmas? G*o to YouTube and search for all the following Seattle International Church Toy Giveaway, Seattle Dream Center Toy Give Away Ray Hampton, Seattle Dream Center Christmas in the City* to check out the Ray Hampton Outreach Ministries Toy Give Away.

151. Thrift Store

Thrift store outreach is a great idea to recycle old merchandise, serve others, and promote the church. Church members can donate clothes and other household items and the church can resell it at an affordable price. Depending on the size of your church, this could be an option for a great outreach in your community!

152. T-Shirts

T-shirts are an easy and affordable outreach idea. You don't even have to sell the shirts; you can give them to your congregation or have each person give a donation to the evangelism and/or outreach ministry. The shirt could say "Ask me about my church", or "How can I pray for you" (Be creative and put you're a phrase on the shirt so people can engage with you, make sure it's a question). Wearing the shirt through-out your city is a good conversation starter and a great way to build future relationships and partnerships with your church.

153.Twitter

Twitter is another effective way of communicating with people that have smartphones, which will connect you with thousands of people by using their Twitter name, such as @DrRayhampton go to Twitter.com to set up your account.

154.Trademark

Trade marking your item will protect anyone from using your name in the state where you live, you can also have your item federally trademark which will protect it within the United States. In either case if someone uses your trademarked item, they must legally pay you for your hard work that you have done, it doesn't matter if they have been saying a certain slogan before you or a piece of clothing with the slogan on it, what really matters, is the one that legally trademarked it. You can trademark things from $100 to a $1500 so why wait when your hundreds of dollars can turn into multi-millions of dollars. If you would like to trademark any items or slogan you may have for your church, ministry or business go to your local Secretary of State online to trademarking.

155.Texting Service

Research shows that in 2022 the number of smartphone users in the world was over 6.648 billion people, which translates to 83.40% of the world population owning a smartphone. In total, the number of people that owns a smart or featurephone is 7.26 billion, making up 91.08% of the world population. You can communicate effectively just by using your cell phone and a mobile texting app, which allows texting from a number you set up on your own that is not connected to your cell phone number, but it's located on your smartphone or tablet you can also use a texting service.

156.Television

Commercial, paid programming and/or local free cable access is a great way to put a visual throughout your community, city, and state to show how your church, ministry or business is actively impacting, empowering, and equipping individuals and families. Before calling the television station the first thing you need to know is how many commercials you would like to run on a weekly and/or monthly schedule. For just a few more dollars, you can even boost up the amplifier on the station, why is boosting important? When your commercial comes on the volume will automatically increase while the viewer is watching. Unless you're a good negotiator, an agent is a great idea to call the station on your behalf of your church, ministry, or business to make sure that you received the best price available on a rotator, which means that your commercial will air throughout the day. All you would have to pay the agency is a percentage of the final cost. Online television is also a great way to market to the social media world and the only cost is the production of the video. Internet television, which is also known as online television, is a digital distribution of television content throughout the Internet. Internet television is a general term that covers the delivery of television shows and other video content over the Internet by video streaming technology, typically through traditional television broadcasters, as opposed to traditional systems like terrestrial, cable and satellite, although Internet itself is received by terrestrial, cable, or satellite methods. Web television is a term used for programs created by a wide variety of companies and individuals for broadcast on Internet television, web television content is produced for broadcast through the World

Wide Web. It is a subset, which is a part of a larger group of related themes of Internet television.

157.Thanksgiving outreach

Thanksgiving is a special time in the United States and traditionally reserved for families. However, not all people have families of their own and many people spend the day alone. You can have volunteers from your church prepare meals for those who don't have family. Seniors, singles, and those in the hospital may be the people who most appreciate the outreach efforts.

158.Talent show

Looking for another opportunity to partner up with local businesses? Would you like to Host a talent show at the church? Businesses can donate services and prizes for winners, and you can get people from all over your community and city to partner with your church, ministry, or business. For every individual, group, musician, or choir that comes to share their talent, they'll bring multiple friends and family members that would come to your church to watch! Advertise the talent show in the local newspaper, set the rules, and bring people together to appreciate an evening of entertainment, fun, food, and fellowship.

159.Tract ministry

A tract which is referred to a brief pamphlet is used for religious purposes. When you are handing a tract to an individual, turn the tract sideways. The reason for turning a tract sideways before you hand it to the receiver, is because most people try to look at it and read what you're handing them but before the receiver starts to read it, they've already received it from your hand. Following are ways to approach people with tracts. As you say the following words

-Here…" I would like you to have this."

- "Did you get one of these?"

- "Here's a special gift for you"

- "This is very valuable and just for you!"

- "You look like you could use some good news!"

- "Here's a FREE GIFT for you"!

The following are just a few ways that will teach you, the where and how to distribute tracts. Tracts are a great evangelism and outreach tool, that will engage the reader to learn about the love of Jesus Christ.

-Anytime you pay for something put some money in the tract

-Leave the tract under your plate before you leave the restaurant

-Don't ask, "Can I give you something to read?" "Most people out of habit will tell you no. But say, "here's something for you to read later"

-In bags of food at your next grocery bag giveaway

-In the pockets of clothing that you're giving away to the homeless

-Inside brand-new pairs of shoes, at your next shoe giveaway

-On top of a paper roll dispenser especially in bathroom stalls

-In an assortment magazine rack and write "Free take One"

-Offer as a lifesaving guide

-Leave on pedestrian cross walks

-On the benches at bus terminals

-Throughout the airport when traveling

-In a hospital waiting room

-Throughout the shopping mall

-Inside books that you are donating

-Hand out throughout your neighborhood

-Dressing rooms at clothing stores

-In napkin dispensers at local restaurants

-Place inside of holiday and birthday cards along with a gift card or cash when handing it to the person or mailing it to them.

-Give out during Harvest season along with the candy

-Attach to helium filled balloons and sent them off

-Leave a generous tip at a restaurant inside of a track

-Inside of handouts at special events

-Between the pages of magazines in waiting rooms

-Inside the literature on airplanes

-At Funeral Homes

-Hand out at sporting events

-Alongside of coffee machines or water coolers at social events

160.Tents for the homeless

The homeless absolutely love tents why? Because a tent feels like they have their own personal shelter. Have members of the congregation purchase some tents and set a time when the outreach team can drive through-out the city to give the tents away. Remember you don't have to build this home you just have to hand it to someone in need!

161.Tarps for the homeless

The homeless absolutely love tents but why do they need a tarp? Because tarps are for at least the following three things; for flooring, to use as covering or to cover the top of the tent. All of three are protection from dampness and rainy days. Have members of the congregation purchase some tarps and set a time when the outreach team can drive through-out the city to give the tarps away.

162.Trash pickup in the community and city

No one likes to see trash on the side of the road. It makes a bad impression on the community. It doesn't matter if you live in the nicest community or city, there are areas that need to be cleaned up. Organizing a trash pick-up group can bring people from all areas of the community. Age is not a factor so it can even be a family event. Create a sign on the side of the road to let the community know your church is organizing the event. Start adopting a block, community, apartment building etc. Today!

163. Underwear for the Homeless

Your church can buy brand new underwear for homeless men and woman and donate the items to some shelters or homeless individuals and families living on the streets. Yes, this is another item just like the socks and shoes that homeless people need the most.

164.Videos online

You can create a YouTube account and keep recorded outreach events online where anyone can watch, upload, and share videos twenty-four hours a day, which will expand your exposure of your church, ministry, or business. It's very important to remember that "what you don't expose will never expand". This can be done by doing the following steps.

1. Go to youtube.com and establish an account
2. Upload three videos to change the status of your account to a channel
3. You can record welcome and or thank you videos to individuals that you have connected with. After giving a general message, have the editor rolled across the lower third of the video the names that you would like to highlight. You can also make the video private and emailed it to individuals or just keep it open for the public.
4. Record and upload every major outreach event that you do in order to gain exposure to your church, ministry or business.

165.Vacation Bible Adventure

Instead of doing your typical summer Vacation Bible School, Let's make it more excited and call it a Vacation Bible Adventure (VBA) program, you could get multiple churches involved and do something amazing! If you combine resources, you might be able to rent a community center or use the building of the largest church. With enough planning, a multi-church community Vacation Bible Adventure (VBA) could make a dramatic impact on the community and even the city! Another plus to a large, multi-church Vacation Bible Adventure (VBA) event is that it lets churches participate even when they have a lot of people vacationing or out for the summer. An outreach idea like this will take many volunteers.

166.Volunteer at a hospital

Become a hospital chaplain or contact the volunteer office for requirements for requirements for ministry opportunities.

167.Volunteer at a nursing home

Become a nursing home chaplain or contact the volunteer office for requirements for ministry opportunities.

168.Volunteer at a community center

This is an amazing outreach for the youth at you're your church. Of course, adults can be excellent volunteers at the community center as well, but the youth are able to engage more with the physical activities. Contact the volunteer office for requirements for ministry opportunities.

169.Volunteer at a school district

Become a volunteer at one of the local schools. Contact the school district office to see were your help is needed the most.

170.Welcome Video

Did you know that you can send every member or customer in your church, ministry or business a PowerPoint? I believe one of the greatest tools that will work for your church, ministries or business that will create exposure and will not leave out any key details that you would want them to know is a PowerPoint presentation. You can create a three-to-seven-page PowerPoint presentation highlighting key photos and events about your church, ministry, or business. Look at the following steps so you or the media team can get started today!

1. Go to slideshare.net and establish an account

2. E-mail the presentation address to each new member.

3. Also post on other social media sites and generate clicks online for your church, ministry, or business

If slide share does not work for you, why don't you try using another website, such as; Animoto.com

1. Go to Animoto.com and establish an account
2. Select eight to twenty photos and add them to the presentation

3. Add your favorite theme or welcome song to the presentation
4. Upload the video to your YouTube account
5. E-mail the link to whoever you would like to receive it

171.Website

The importance of having a website is to keep everyone informed across the United States and internationally about updates of your church, ministry, or business. There are three things that are very important in keeping your website informative.

1. A mission statement
2. A vision statement
3. The purpose and core values of your church, ministry, or business

Your structure plan needs to be simple with clarity but effective. If possible, don't use a Gmail, Hotmail, or etc. for your e-mail address. Always have an e-mail address that matches your website, because most of the time people will not treat your organization seriously. Build your own website for free by going online to a free website builder or you can have it professionally done. Many website builders will be able to host your website for economical fee depending on, how long you want them to host it for, they also will provide you with a certain amount of emails that are free that will be identical to your website. Remember, when everything matches it gives your church, ministry, or business a professional look!

172. Walk-a-thon

There are always people in need. It may be first responders who need support, or families fighting cancer, or a tragic event like a home that was burned to the ground. A walk-a-thon is an outreach opportunity that helps the community and gets people involved. Keep an eye on the newspaper in your area and look for walk-a-thon opportunities to help others. This activity can be a one-time event or a frequent initiative for the community.

173. Yard Sale

Here's an outreach idea that doubles up on the opportunity to reach out to your community. Think of something meaningful in your community you'd like to raise money for and put together a community-wide yard sale to raise funds. As an outreach, it's best if you're not just fundraising for your own needs. The people in the community and city get to come interact with you, when they donate their sale items to the yard sale, and then they get to interact with your church again when they come to the actual event! Don't underestimate the number of volunteer hours that will need to go into sorting, cleaning, and pricing the items that people bring. It's time-consuming, but worth it!

174. Youth Mission Trip

Missions trips have always been an exciting opportunity for church youth. Whether the opportunity is building a house in Mexico or cleaning up after a devastating hurricane, a mission trip educates youth to the world and helps others. Mission trips don't have to be far away, they can be in your local community where help is needed. Remember, while you're planning on going oversees to help, make sure that you're not 'over seeing' the needs in your own community and city. So, before you decide to go help abroad (somewhere else), serve locally.

175. Zoom

Zoom meetings has the ability to reach those who may not be able to attend in person events due to transportation, schedule conflicts or health reasons. Thousands of churches, ministries and business have successfully used zoom for weekly church services, staff and volunteer meetings, as well as online teachings.

12 MONTH MINISTRY ACTION PLAN (M.A.P)

1st Quarter

January-March

January

In-reach: Light up a life service, paying partial or full utility bills through drawings.

Outreach: Coat, jackets, and sweaters to the homeless.

February

In-reach: Date night for couples.

Outreach: Tarp and/or blanket giveaway to the homeless.

March

In-reach: Grocery giveaway to individuals and families.

Outreach: Feeding the homeless and hungry.

2nd Quarter

April-May

April

In-reach: Celebration service.

Outreach: Gas Giveaway or community/city egg hunt, with food and drawings for gifts.

May

In-reach: Mother's Day celebration service.

Outreach: Hygiene Packs to the homeless.

June

In-reach: Father's Day celebration service.

Outreach: Community or City ice cream social.

3rd Quarter

June-August

July

In-reach: Vacation Bible Adventure for children (Summer vacation bible school).

Outreach: Sack Lunch/Dinner feeding the homeless and hungry.

August

In-reach: Children's celebration service.

Outreach: Backpack and School supplies giveaway to children.

September

In-reach: Invite to Church celebration service.

Outreach: Shoe giveaway to children.

4th Quarter

October-December

October

In-reach: Harvest Party.

Outreach: Socks and blanket giveaway to the homeless.

November

In-reach: Thanksgiving celebration service.

Outreach: Thanksgiving grocery bag giveaway.

December

In-reach: Christmas Celebration service.

Outreach: Toy giveaway to children.

Dr. Ray Hampton's Biography

In July 1991, at the age of twenty-six, Dr. Ray Hampton realized that he had a passion to help people in a great way, so he went out on the street corner to start reaching the homeless, hopeless, helpless and hungry. For thirty-two years and counting, many outreaches have been extended to children and adults, such as; "Christmas in the City" over 104,145 toys has been distributed, "Back to School" over 19,145 backpacks filled with school supplies and hundreds of thousands of meals to individuals and families experiencing food insecurities. These are just a few of the many outreaches.

He's a Certified Registered Chaplin, entrepreneur, television personality, public figure, and author. He's also a mentor to National Football League players, chief executive officers. He also serves as an evangelism and outreach growth consultant to many leaders, pastors and churches throughout the United States teaching people how to engage, be equipped and empowered for evangelism and outreach.

Dr. Ray Hampton believes in higher education, having started out at Washington State University and continued his education at A. L. Hardy Academy of Theology. To his acclaim, he currently holds a master's degree in marriage and biblical family counseling and two doctoral degrees, one in ministry and the other in theology. Dr. Hampton currently lives in Fort Lauderdale, Florida, with his wife, Julia, whom he married at seventeen years old. They have been married for 40 years and have raised ten children. He continues to provide answers to problems by serving with his palms down and not his palms up.

Made in the USA
Middletown, DE
11 August 2024